Rock, A Life Story

THE ILLUSTRATED ENCYCLOPEDIA OF ALBUMS, ARTISTS AND GREAT SONGS

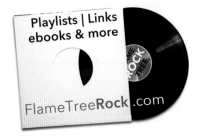

This is a **FLAME TREE** book
First published 2013

Publisher and Creative Director: Nick Wells
Senior Project Editor: Catherine Taylor
Picture Research: Emma Chafer, Esme Chapman and Catherine Taylor
Art Director: Michael Spender
Layout Design: Michael Spender
Proofreader: Julia Rolf

This edition first published 2013 by
FLAME TREE PUBLISHING
Crabtree Hall, Crabtree Lane
Fulham, London SW6 6TY
United Kingdom

www.flametreepublishing.com

3 5 7 9 10 8 6 4 2
15 17 16 14

ISBN 978-0-85775-807-1

A CIP record for this book is available from the British Library upon request.

Printed in China

Rock, A Life Story

THE ILLUSTRATED ENCYCLOPEDIA OF ALBUMS, ARTISTS AND GREAT SONGS

Foreword by Brian May • Consultant Editor: Paul du Noyer

Contributing authors: Michael Heatley, Kylie Olsson, Richard Buskin, Alan Clayson, Joe Cushley, Rusty Cutchin, Jason Draper, Hugh Fielder, Mike Gent, Drew Heatley, Jake Kennedy, Colin Salter, Ian Shirley, John Tobler

FLAME TREE PUBLISHING

Contents

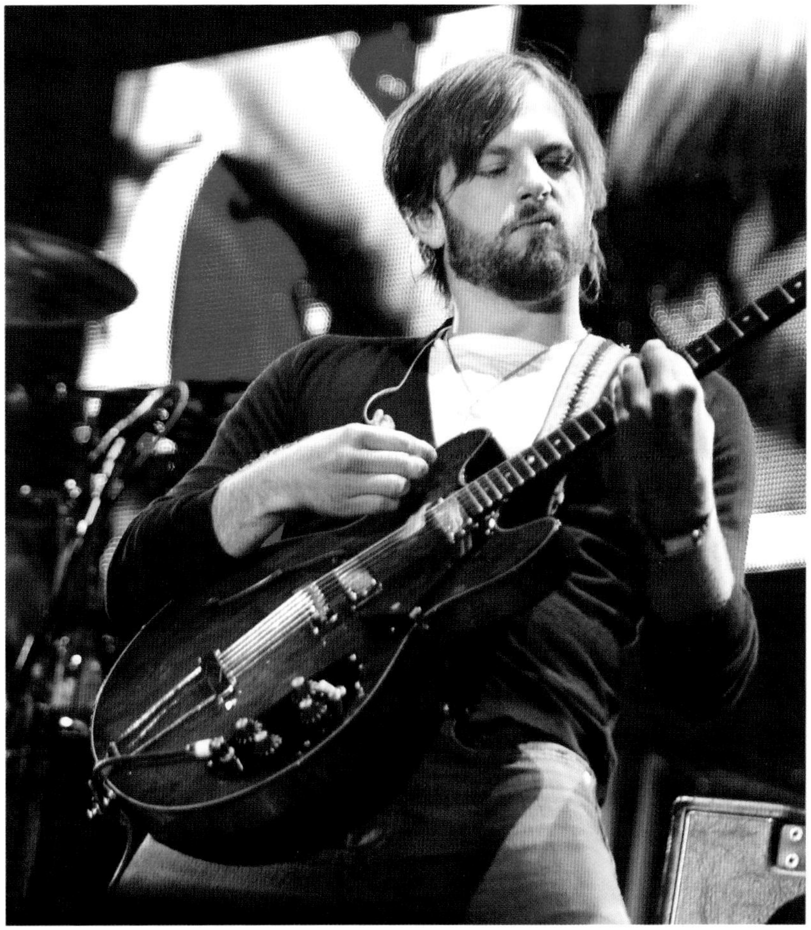

Many Stories

"I hope I die before I get old..."

The Who, ''talkin' 'bout their generation' in 1965. *Their* generation then is *ours still*: the story of rock, with its kaleidoscope of artists, sounds, gigs and media, is driven now by the twin forces of youthful rebellion and, increasingly, a vibrant sense of nostalgia for those of us who have lived and loved music for our entire lives.

Rock, A Life Story starts with the explosion of the Fifties and races through to the complex scene of the Twenty-First Century where music rolls around our daily lives in stores, online, on social media and through every form of entertainment. In the inklings, at the birth of rock, nobody could have imagined that the music of rebellion would remain with us, morphing with each new generation of adolescents. The Stones still perform world tours well into their dotage, bands from the Seventies, Eighties and Nineties constantly reform because their market has not fallen away, merely changed its style of clothing.

The book does not set out to be a *definitive* history and compendium of rock, rather, it takes you on a journey that highlights significant developments and features the 'headline acts' of each decade. It will take you back to those milestone moments in your own life – your first LP perhaps, that early Led Zepp gig, the first time you heard a song on the radio or the internet, a mixtape you made for your friends. And for some it will bring the rush of the new.

It is impossible to cover every singer, band and album, so, **Rock, A Life Story** offers a self-conscious highlight of the sights, sounds and the best acts of the rock era. That means we've left out a great many artists, bands, producers and performers. So, we've set up a website, **FlameTreeRock.com** to cover much of this missing territory.

FlameTreeRock.com offers a very wide range of other resources for your interest and entertainment:

1. **Extensive lists** and **links to artists**, organized by decade: Sixties, Seventies and more.
2. **Free ebooks** with the story of other musical genres, such as soul, R&B, disco, rap & Hip Hop.
3. **Special features** on the many **styles of rock**: what is the difference between Heavy Metal and Nu Metal, Grindcore and Grunge?
4. **Mixtape selections** from every era, to give you the sounds of each generation of rock music.
5. **YouTube** video selections of the top artists and their great performances.

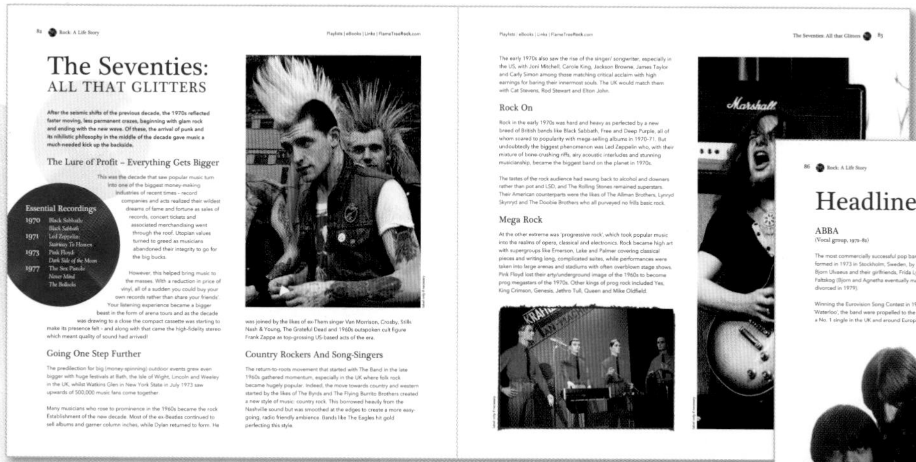

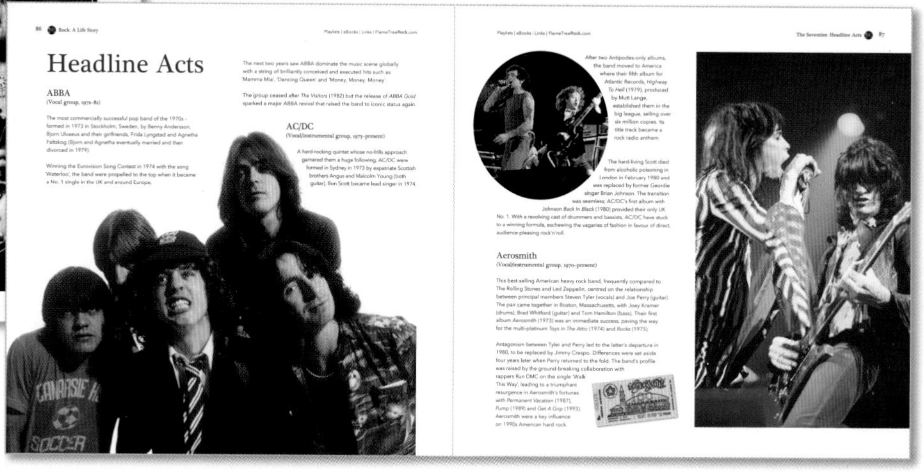

Foreword

***Rock, A Life Story* is something of a well-organized scrapbook of memories of rock, from its birth in the 1950s to the place it occupies in the twenty-first century as a culture that inspires and involves *all* generations.**

I'm lucky enough to have been around at the birth of rock'n'roll – as a kid born at the end of the 1940s, and coming into awareness in the 1950s. My first chills up the spine occurred as I secretly listened to Radio Luxembourg on my homemade crystal set radio with headphones – under the covers, when I was supposed to be sleeping. The sounds I heard have echoed in my head my whole life through, and inspired me to make music the central thread of my existence. I can chart my growth as a person through the history of rock music.

To us ol' post-war baby-boomers, this book, picked up and flicked through in quiet moments, will gently jog our memories, reopen those precious pathways in our brains that preserve the soundtrack of our lives. For those who entered the story of rock later on, some of these early colourful snapshots will make you feel like you were there all along, sharing that excitement, feeling that beat.

And for all of us, here is an entertaining overview of a life … a life in rock. Turn the pages, enjoy the words and pictures, and feel the pulse of a phenomenon that changed the world – when kids seized the chance to voice and share their passion. Those kids grew into the world of adults, but the spirit of rock never grows old … it just keeps on growing.

Enjoy!

Brian May

Introduction

The secret of rock music's survival over the past sixty years is its seemingly limitless capacity to re-invent itself. The one constant is that it is essentially the music of rebellious youth. As each generation enters its teens, it needs its own music to help define itself. And, as each generation enters adulthood, it takes with it those 'teenage dreams so hard to beat' and the music that helped shape them.

Just as the rock'n'roll of the 1950s was a rebellion against the swing and jazz of the previous decade, so every successive sub-genre of rock has been a reaction against the previous generation's definition of it. This inspired an endless succession of different styles: rock'n'roll, British invasion, psychedelia, prog rock, punk, heavy metal (and its many variants), new romantic, Britpop, indie ... the list is endless.

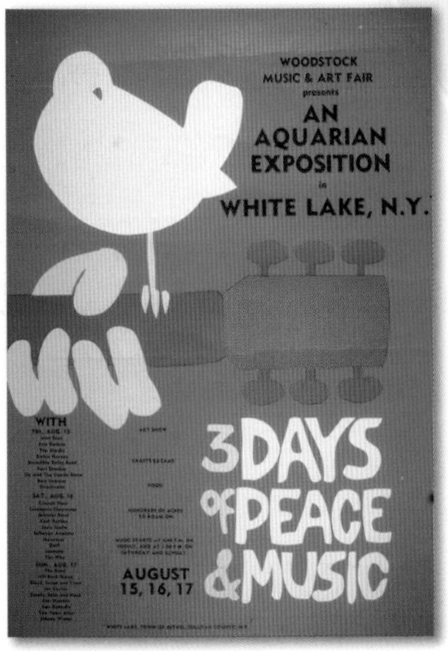

From Festivals To Film

There have traditionally been two ways in which pop and rock can be accessed: live performance and recordings. In the 1950s a proliferation of dance halls and folk clubs let young bands hone their performing skills; when they achieved popularity, package tours gave bands such as The Beatles national exposure. The end of the 1960s brought the rock festival's inexorable rise, starting with Monterey in 1967, the iconic Woodstock two years later and the Isle of Wight festival (1968–70, 2002–present). Festivals today are big business. Glastonbury, founded in 1970, leads in Britain, with America's Coachella and Lollopalooza both equally massive events, while rock is also regularly played in outdoor sports stadia.

Despite the number of festivals, big and small, that exist nowadays, not everyone can afford to attend them, so recorded performances have always been a cheaper and more accessible alternative. Rock'n'roll first entered the public's consciousness when 'Rock Around The Clock' was featured in the film *Blackboard Jungle* in 1955. Since then rock music and movies have been inextricably linked, through the films of Elvis Presley, The Beatles' innovative *A Hard Day's Night*, *Saturday Night Fever* (which brought disco to the world) and a host of 'chick flicks' such as *Pretty Woman* and *Dirty Dancing*. And, of course, this association of audio and video paved the way, when the technology was right in the 1980s, for the rise of the ubiquitous music video.

Reaching The Masses

In the 1950s the newly invented 45rpm vinyl single quickly usurped the shellac 78 on coffee-bar jukeboxes or auto-change Dansette record players at home. In Britain, national radio stations were simply not rock-oriented; the alternative was the fading late-night broadcasts of Radio Luxembourg. BBC television had the *Six-Five Special* in the 1950s and *Top Of The Pops,* which reigned supreme from 1964 until satellite TV killed it off in 2006, but these were glorious exceptions. The pirate radio ships of the mid-1960s offered an exciting new alternative and the BBC eventually caught up in 1967 with the launch of Radio 1.

During the 1960s the pre-eminence of the 7-inch, 45rpm single was eroded by the 12-inch long-playing record, as the 33-and-a-third-revolutions-per-minute album came into its own. Cassette tapes also appeared during the decade, and these became a convenient method of making and storing home-produced compilations. The home consumer could 'cherry-pick' their favourite tracks, the start of a trend that is still with us in the shape of iTunes. This has inevitably eroded the pre-eminence of the album in favour of the single once more. Nowadays a new album release by a band such as Coldplay or U2 is just a curtain-raiser to the release of singles extracted from it.

Mark Knopfler of Dire Straits

Vinyl And Cassettes Lose Out

The long-playing vinyl record reigned supreme throughout the 1970s until the mid-1980s, when the compact disc was marketed. Although seen initially as a rich person's toy that would soon lose its appeal, it wasn't long before the CD loosened and, eventually, overthrew vinyl's stranglehold on the music industry. This was helped in part by Dire Straits' *Brothers In Arms*, not only one of the first albums to be recorded digitally (in 1984) but also one of the first to be directed at the CD market for release. Although the smaller size of the CD – five inches square as against the twelve inches square vinyl – was more convenient for home storage, it also meant that album artwork was reduced to a shadow of its former self.

The other big revolution in how music was accessed and enjoyed was the advent of music television delivered to the world's living room via satellite. MTV was launched in the States in 1981 and made stars of bands with the visual style to complement their music. A video to accompany a single was now obligatory, while the solo career of Michael Jackson was considerably accelerated by his *Thriller* clip – in effect a mini-movie. The pre-recorded music DVD, the successor to VHS video, found success in the wake of this audio-visual revolution, but has since dipped in popularity due to internet streaming and is in danger of being eclipsed by the Blu-Ray format.

The Digital Drive

As home computers became ubiquitous during the 1990s it was inevitable that methods of musical delivery would catch up. Not only could songs be stored on hard disk as MP3 files, they could be downloaded via the internet from websites dedicated to the task. The first iPod was introduced in 2001 and, just as the CD had spelt the death sentence for vinyl albums, the new digital device threatened to relegate CDs to specialist collector status. Apple computers made more money from iPods than from selling computers and this simple device, the successor to the cassette-based (and later CD-based) Sony Walkman of the 1980s, allowed consumers to store their entire music library on a device no bigger than a matchbox.

Record retailers bore the brunt of this shift, Britain's HMV chain going under in 2013 – another area of shared musical enjoyment had been consigned to history as certainly as the 'listening booths'

in the record shops of yesteryear. Digital and internet radio also took off in the twenty-first century, with the result that every conceivable musical taste is now catered for. No more crowding round the transistor radio on Sunday nights to find out the No.1 for the coming week, although downloading has inspired new interest in the singles chart due to the consumer's instant ability to influence it. By means of social media campaigns, the most unlikely releases can become overnight hits.

Today we are living in a world where music has never been so accessible. Almost any track from the past sixty years can be instantly called up on the internet along with its video or live performance on YouTube. Digital streaming programmes such as Spotify are like twenty-first-century 'global jukeboxes', a cornucopia of musical riches available at the click of a mouse.

So what will tomorrow's rock music sound like? There is no way of knowing until it arrives – but you can be sure that the younger generation will instantly recognize it and, inevitably, their parents will dismiss it. That, after all, is what rock music is for. But for those who take the time to listen, it will still have the same vibrancy and energy that helped shape rock'n'roll half a century or more ago.

Lady Gaga

'We like this kind of music. Jazz is strictly for stay-at-homes.'

Buddy Holly on rock'n'roll

Roots

Roots:
THE BUILDING BLOCKS OF ROCK

Rock'n'roll did not spring fully formed from Memphis in the shape of Elvis Presley but was a fusion of many genres, principally rhythm & blues and country. The former was an urban black phenomenon, the latter a rural white one.

Ebony And Ivory

Bill Haley helped blur the line between black and white when his cover of bluesman Joe Turner's 'Shake, Rattle And Roll' became an early rock'n'roll anthem in 1954.

Conversely, black vocal groups like The Dominoes and The Orioles released harmony-coated hits 'Sixty Minute Man' (1951) and 'Crying In The Chapel' (1953) which appealed to a white audience.

From the 1930s, country music was broadcast on American radio from the Grand Ole Opry in Nashville. The Delmore Brothers, a hillbilly duo, drew on Appalachian folk and more uptempo boogie-woogie material. By the end of 1947, they used electric guitars and drums.

Essential Recordings

1931 Jimmie Rodgers: *Mule Skinner Blues*
1948 Muddy Waters: *I Can't Be Satisfied*
1955 Little Richard: *Tutti Frutti*
1956 Elvis Presley: *Hound Dog*
1957 The Everly Brothers: *Wake Up Little Susie*
1958 Chuck Berry: *Johnny B. Goode*

Let The Good Times Roll

When he founded Sun Records in Memphis, Sam Phillips needed a white singer who could sing the blues. He believed this would break down the musical colour divide. That man, of course, was Elvis Presley, whose story appears later in this book. Although Phillips eventually sold Elvis Presley's contract to RCA Victor, he still had Jerry Lee Lewis, Carl Perkins and Johnny Cash, all of whom enjoyed long and influential careers.

Teenager In Love

After the depression of the 1930s, a new post-war generation of white youth emerged to whom wartime austerity was anathema. Films like James Dean's *Rebel Without A Cause* (1955) gave them their first role models.

While traditional composers had written about romance from an adult viewpoint, rock's new songwriters now addressed teenage subjects in their lyrics for the first time.

Chuck Berry's songs of romance, frustration and homework crossed the colour and gender divides, and the Brill Building turned out quality pop from the pens of tunesmiths like Neil Sedaka and Carole King.

Joe Turner

The Rock'n'Roll Gospel

The rock'n'roll gospel was spread by DJ Alan Freed, instigator of a number of 'rock exploitation' movies, and Dick Clark, whose *American Bandstand* TV show from Philadelphia spawned the likes of Frankie Avalon, Fabian and Bobby Rydell. All were fresh-faced Italian-American teen idols with varying degrees of natural talent. A series of US 'heart-throb' male singers, such as Paul Anka, Ricky Nelson and Pat Boone, also emerged around this time.

Singing For Britain

Britain began its rock'n'roll odyssey via the skiffle boom led by Lonnie Donegan. It provided the training ground for many of Britain's rock names of the late 1950s and 1960s, who started their musical careers playing acoustic guitar, tea-chest bass or home-made percussion; the electric guitar was still a rarity.

Cliff Richard towered above all other British acts at this time. Jack Good's TV show, *Oh Boy!*, gave Cliff and backing group The Shadows their passport to stardom, courtesy of the single 'Move It'.

As far as the 1950s went, America seemed to hold all the aces, but British beat, and The Beatles, had a card or two up their sleeve.

Skiffle group

'Let's face it – rock'n'roll is bigger than all of us.'

Alan Freed

Alan Freed

Headline Acts

Chet Atkins

(Guitar, producer, 1924–2001)

Tennessee-born Chester Burton Atkins, whose father was a music teacher, was one of the most influential twentieth-century guitarists, and was initially influenced by the finger- and thumb-picking country-style playing of Merle Travis. Signed to RCA from 1947, he made scores of mainly instrumental albums, and in 1955 became the head of RCA's new Nashville studio, producing artists signed to the label, and working with numerous country artists including Don Gibson, Waylon Jennings, Elvis Presley and Jim Reeves. He also produced for pop artists such as Perry Como, and was recognized by Gretsch guitars, who named their Chet Atkins Country Gentleman model after him. One of his most significant signings to RCA was successful black country singer Charley Pride, as few black acts were tolerated in Nashville. Atkins also made duet albums with notable pickers like Les Paul, Jerry Reed and Mark Knopfler (1992's *Neck And Neck*).

Chuck Berry

(Guitar, singer/songwriter, b. 1926)

Charles Edward Anderson Berry was born in St Louis, Missouri, in 1926. He began learning the guitar in his mid-teens but at 17 was involved in a string of robberies leading to a stint in jail, where he stayed until his twenty-first birthday.

On release, Berry played gigs wherever he could. He was used to playing white bars, and started to introduce country songs alongside blues numbers and standards. While Elvis was a hillbilly singer who sang the blues, Berry was a bluesman who sang hillbilly. They both ended up with the same result: rock'n'roll.

In early 1955, Muddy Waters recommended that he should see Leonard Chess. The head of Chess Records liked the sound of Berry's 'Ida May', which he had developed from Bob Wills's 'Ida Red', but he cautiously advised further disguise. The song became 'Maybellene'. It appealed to all tastes and stormed up the American charts in 1955, reaching No. 5 on the *Billboard* chart several months before Elvis appeared as a national star.

Essential Recordings

- **1955** *Maybellene*
- **1956** *Roll Over Beethoven, Too Much Monkey Business*
- **1958** *Sweet Little Sixteen, Johnny B. Goode*
- **1963** *Chuck Berry*
- **1964** *Nadine, No Particular Place To Go, You Never Can Tell*
- **1965** *The Promised Land*
- **1971** *San Francisco Dues*
- **1972** *My Ding-A-Ling*

Chet Atkins

Berry's band began touring and, around this time, he started performing his trademark duck walk across stage. In mid-1956, 'Roll Over Beethoven' entered the US Top 30. 'School Days' became a smash hit in 1957, reaching No. 3 in the US and giving Berry his first UK hit. Berry was in his thirties, but could describe teenage life to a tee.

After School Sessions was both Berry and Chess Records' first LP, released in 1958. 'Sweet Little Sixteen' climbed to No. 2 in the US, and No. 16 in the UK. 'Johnny B. Goode' came next, reaching No. 8 in America.

In 1959 his chart placings began to slip. After bringing a 14-year-old Apache girl from Mexico to work at his St Louis club, Berry spent two more years in jail for 'transporting a minor for immoral purposes'. However, he put his time inside to good use: writing a selection of songs that would re-establish him.

Chuck had a string of hits in the UK, including 'Memphis, Tennessee', 'No Particular Place To Go', 'Nadine', 'Run, Rudolph, Run' and 'You Never Can Tell'. Both The Beatles and The Rolling Stones were heavily influenced by him: The Stones' first single 'Come On' was a Chuck original. In May 1964, Berry toured the UK to a tumultuous reception.

In 1972 he recorded a live gig in Coventry that resulted in his biggest, but by no means finest, hit. 'My Ding-A-Ling', a risqué novelty number written by Dave Bartholomew, was a transatlantic No. 1.

Berry ended the 1970s in jail again on tax charges. In 1986, he was inducted into the Rock And Roll Hall Of Fame by Keith Richards, who based a career on Berry's guitar style. The same year Richards organized a sixtieth birthday bash for him, filmed in its entirety as the documentary *Hail! Hail! Rock'n'Roll*; a fascinating tribute to a great showman and a huge influence on all who followed.

'[My mama] said, "You and Elvis are pretty good, but you're no Chuck Berry."'

Jerry Lee Lewis

Chuck Berry

Johnny Cash

Johnny Cash

(Guitar, singer/songwriter, 1932–2003)

Arkansas-born Cash enjoyed a 49-year career involving several periods of huge popularity. After USAF service, he formed a trio with Luther Perkins (guitar) and Marshall Chapman (bass). Auditioning for Sam Phillips at Sun Records in Memphis, Cash played rockabilly. He scored more than 20 US country hits and several US pop hits before signing with Columbia/CBS in late 1958, when he became among the biggest country music attractions, remaining with the label until 1987. Cash became an American treasure during the 1960s, particularly after recording live albums *At Folsom Prison* (1968) and *At San Quentin* (1969), which both went triple platinum. In 1968, he married June Carter (of The Carter Family), and they fronted a hugely popular live revue for many years. After 1976, further mainstream success seemed an impossibility, until producer Rick Rubin offered to produce him; 1994's *American Recordings* was the first of four Grammy-winning albums on Rubin's label. Cash's daughter, Rosanne, keeps the Cash name popular.

Ray Charles

(Piano, singer/songwriter, 1930–2004)

Ray Charles Robinson was born in 1930 in Albany, Georgia. He was blind from the age of seven and attended the Institute for the Blind, Deaf and Dumb in St Augustine, Florida, where he learned to play piano, organ, clarinet and saxophone and to read music in Braille.

Charles started his musical career gigging around Jacksonville, Orlando and Tampa, and began modelling himself on the smooth style of Nat 'King' Cole.

He moved to Seattle in March 1948 and landed a recording contract with Jack Lauderdale's Downbeat label. His debut single, 'Confession Blues' (1949), became an R&B hit. Three years later, Lauderdale sold Ray's contract to Atlantic Records.

Ray's first recording session for Atlantic was in 1952. His first few singles were only minor hits, but in November 1954 he recorded 'I Got A Woman'. The tune was based on a gospel song and laid the groundwork for soul music. Tracks such as 'Hallelujah I Love Her So' and 'What'd I Say' built on this foundation.

Ray Charles

In 1959 Ray Charles recorded jazz on *The Genius Of Ray Charles* (1959). In 1960, he signed to ABC-Paramount and founded his own record label, Tangerine. He achieved chart success with a pair of US No. 1s, 'Georgia On My Mind' and 'Hit The Road Jack'.

In 1962 he produced the crossover classic *Modern Sounds In Country And Western Music* (1962), which became his only US No. 1 album, and yielded another chart-topping single in 'I Can't Stop Loving You'.

Charles died on 10 June 2004. His posthumous album *Genius Loves Company* (2004) featured duets with Gladys Knight, Willie Nelson and Norah Jones, while Jamie Foxx won an Oscar playing him in the Hollywood biopic *Ray* (2004).

Eddie Cochran

(Guitar, singer/songwriter, 1938–60)

Oklahoma-born Cochran was a rising star of rock'n'roll, guest-starring in 1956's *The Girl Can't Help It*, the best ever rock'n'roll movie. He wrote songs with lyrics that spoke to teenagers like 1958's 'Summertime Blues' (US Top 10/UK Top 20) and 1959's 'C'mon Everybody' (UK Top 10). After dying in a car crash while on tour in Britain with Gene Vincent, his UK popularity increased, with 1960's 'Three Steps To Heaven' topping the UK charts. After Presley and Holly, Cochran is probably the best-loved US rock'n'roll star in Britain, and among his other hits were 1959's 'Teenage Heaven' and 'Somethin' Else', and his excellent cover of the Ray Charles classic 'Hallelujah I Love Her So'. 1960's *Eddie Cochran Memorial Album* made the Top 10 of the UK album chart.

Bo Diddley

(Guitar, vocals, 1928–2008)

Born Ellas Bates in McComb, Mississippi, Bo Diddley developed his guitar skills and stage persona in Chicago. He had his first guitar by the age of 10. By 1951, at 23, he was a regular in clubs on Chicago's South Side. By 1955 he was signed to Checker, a spinoff of Chess Records. His debut single was a two-sided gem that featured his compositions 'Bo Diddley' and 'I'm A Man'.

The single gave the world the 'Bo Diddley beat', a staccato rhythm that was picked up and used in hits by Buddy Holly ('Not Fade Away') and The Who ('Magic Bus'), among others. Diddley was also known for his 'cigar box' guitar, which he first designed and built in 1945 while at school. Diddley's songs, like 'You Don't Love Me', 'Pretty Thing', 'Diddy Wah Diddy', 'Who Do You Love?' and 'Mona', reflect the energy and drive of early rock'n'roll.

Fats Domino

(Piano, singer/songwriter, b. 1928)

Signed to Imperial Records, New Orleans-born Antoine Domino's first million-seller, 'The Fat Man' (1949) began a run of over 60 US pop and R&B hits by 1964, many written by Domino with Dave Bartholomew. Other million-selling classics included 'Ain't That A Shame' (1955), 'Bo Weevil', 'I'm In Love Again' and 'Blueberry Hill (all 1956), 'Blue Monday' (featured in *The Girl Can't Help It*) and 'I'm Walkin'' (both 1957) and 'Whole Lotta Loving' (1958). Domino's secret appears to be that he has never changed, his smoky Louisiana accent above his percussive piano-playing making him instantly recognizable. Twist king Ernest Evans used the name Chubby Checker in polite emulation. Domino's last US hit was a 1968 cover of 'Lady Madonna' by The Beatles, who apparently wrote the song in Domino's style. In September 2005 Domino made international news bulletins when his house was destroyed by Hurricane Katrina, but he happily survived.

Lonnie Donegan

(Guitar, singer/songwriter, 1931–2002)

Born Anthony James Donegan in Glasgow, Lonnie was single-handedly responsible for the British skiffle boom of the 1950s. He blended elements of various American roots songs, often employing improvised instruments such as a tea-chest bass and washboard. He released Leadbelly's 'Rock Island Line' as a single in late 1955; it went to No. 8 in the UK, and reached the same position in the US charts.

'Cumberland Gap' was his first No. 1 in 1957 and there followed 'Gamblin' Man', 'The Grand Coolee Dam' and 'Tom Dooley'. He then introduced numbers rooted in British music-hall traditions, such as 'Does Your Chewing Gum Lose Its Flavour (On The Bedpost Overnight)?' (1959) and 'My Old Man's A Dustman' (1960, another UK chart-topper). Although some saw this as a cheapening of his act, Donegan was highly influential on many British rock artists and, towards the end of his life, was seen as the 'Grand Old Man' of British rock.

Fats Domino

Duane Eddy
(Guitar, b. 1938)

With producer/co-writer Lee Hazlewood, Eddy scored 20 US hits between 1958 and 1961, showcasing his 'twangy' guitar on the Jamie label, part-owned by Hazlewood. Eddy's US Top 10 hits were 1958's 'Rebel Rouser', 1959's 'Forty Miles Of Bad Road' and 1960's 'Because They're Young'. After signing with RCA in 1962, his appeal largely left him, his biggest hit being 1962's US Top 20 '(Dance With The) Guitar Man'. After a 20-year plus US chart absence, he returned in 1986 as featured instrumentalist on a revival of his 1960 'Peter Gunn' hit by The Art Of Noise.

Duane Eddy

The Everly Brothers
(Vocal duo, Don Everly b. 1937. Phil Everly b. 1939)

The Everlys were born into a country music family; Don in Brownie, Kentucky, Phil in Chicago. The family had a regular show on local radio in Shenandoah, Iowa.

After moving to Knoxville, Tennessee, the boys' father Ike used his friendship with Chet Atkins to get them introduced to Wesley Rose of the Acuff-Rose publishing partnership. Rose got them a deal with the Cadence label.

The brothers teamed up with songwriting couple Felice and Boudleaux Bryant, and in mid-1957 'Bye Bye Love' reached No. 2 in the US, 6 in the UK. There followed 'Wake Up Little Susie' (1957), 'All I Have To Do Is Dream', 'Bird Dog' (both 1958) and their first self-penned hit '('Til) I Kissed You' (1959).

A bitter split with manager Wesley Rose heralded a move to the newly founded Warner Brothers label on a million-dollar 10-year contract.

Their first offering at the new label was 'Cathy's Clown' (1960). The Beatles would later admit they had based the arrangement of 'Please Please Me' on this track. Further big sellers ensued in 'Lucille' (1960), 'Walk Right Back' and innovative pop epic 'Temptation' (both 1961). But trouble was looming: Don became reliant on drugs; the British invasion stole their chart thunder; and their bust-up with Rose meant that they had trouble getting songs from the best Nashville writers.

They drifted on until July 1973, when a drunken Don insulted his brother on-stage. Long-running grievances erupted, and the normally placid Phil stormed off. They did not play together again for 10 years. It took their father's funeral in 1983 to reconcile them. They continue to tour and record to this day, their considerable powers undiminished.

Bill Haley
(Guitar, vocals, 1925–1981)

William John Clifton Haley was born in Highland Park, Detroit, and raised in Pennsylvania. He got his first guitar when he was 13. Even though he was blind in one eye and shy about his disability, he started playing local shows.

After playing in a variety of country & western bands, Haley landed a job on radio station WPWA in Chester, forming The Saddlemen. Here he first heard 'Rocket 88' by Jackie Brenston and His Delta Cats and recorded it in 1951 with The Saddlemen: the first cover of the first

Bill Haley

rock'n'roll record. The band signed to the Essex label where, as Bill Haley with Haley's Comets, 'Crazy Man Crazy,' became the first charting rock'n'roll record in history, reaching No. 15.

Decca signed Haley in April 1954. They spent most of the session working on 'Thirteen Women', allowing only two takes for B-side 'Rock Around The Clock'. The track was more popular than the A-side but was not a big hit. Instead Haley went to No. 12 in the summer of 1954 with 'Shake Rattle And Roll', which also became his first UK hit. The film producer of *Blackboard Jungle* chose 'Rock Around The Clock' to capture the mood of disaffected youth in the movie; when it came out in 1955, the track shot to No. 1 and stayed there for eight weeks.

Haley and his band had further big hits with 'Rock-A-Beatin' Boogie' (1955), 'See You Later, Alligator' and 'The Saints Rock'n'Roll' (both 1956), and toured Britain in 1957.

Haley's last US hit came in late 1959 with 'Skokiaan (The South African Song)'. He managed a final British gig at the Royal Variety Performance in late 1979, but, after suffering from a brain tumour, died in February 1981.

Buddy Holly

(Guitar, vocals 1936–59)

Charles Hardin Holley (its original spelling) was born in Lubbock, Texas, in 1936. He got a guitar in his mid-teens and started practising country and blues. Guitarist Sonny Curtis, bassist Don Guess and drummer Jerry Allison joined him to form The Crickets after he secured a deal with Decca in Nashville.

Things didn't work out, so Holly returned to Norman Petty's studio in Clovis, New Mexico, where he had previously recorded demos.

'That'll Be The Day' became the The Crickets' first hit. It went to the US No. 1 in summer 1957. Thereafter tracks were alternately credited to The Crickets or Buddy Holly, doubling the chances of airplay. 'Peggy Sue', 'Oh Boy' backed with 'Not Fade Away', 'Maybe Baby', 'Listen To Me' and 'Rave On' were all big hits. Meanwhile, the band toured with Chuck Berry, The Everlys and Fats Domino, amongst many others. 'Words Of Love' was taken from the *Buddy Holly* album, released in March 1958 (July 1958, UK), and 'Peggy Sue' from *The Chirping Crickets* in November 1957 (March 1958 in the UK). Both used pioneering overdubbing and double-tracking techniques.

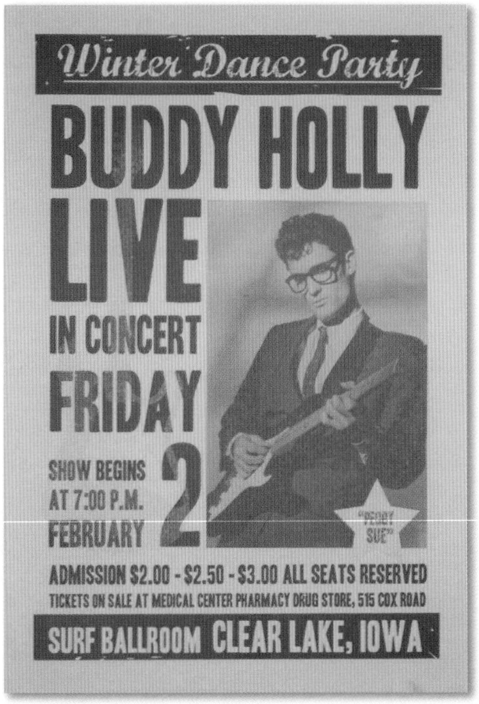

Holly recorded some tracks with a string orchestra in October 1958: 'True Love Ways', and the two songs which would make up his final single, 'It Doesn't Matter Anymore' and 'Raining In My Heart'. Later in October, Holly and Petty went their separate ways although The Crickets stayed with Norman.

In the new year, Buddy got a band together to headline the 'Winter Dance Party' tour. After a gig at Clear Lake, Iowa, Holly, Ritchie Valens and the Big Bopper died when a chartered plane crashed in snowy conditions on 3 February 1959.

So much potential unfulfilled, but a legacy left that would influence generations of rockers and singer/songwriters.

John Lee Hooker
(Guitar, vocals, 1917–2001)

As a youth in Mississippi blues superstar John Lee Hooker was exposed to blues musicians by his stepfather. After living in Memphis and Cincinnati he gravitated to Detroit in 1943, where he recorded the single 'Boogie Chillen'. It reached the top of the R&B charts in 1948. Follow-ups included the hits 'Hobo Blues', 'Hoogie Boogie' and 'Crawling King Snake Blues'.

Throughout the 1950s Hooker often recorded under pseudonyms like Delta John, Birmingham Sam and Little Pork Chops.

Hooker's mournful voice and droning guitar had an enormous influence on British rock bands like The Yardbirds and The Animals, who covered his 'Boom Boom' in 1964. Hooker continued label-hopping through the 1960s and had a major success with 1970's *Hooker 'n' Heat*, teaming with the band Canned Heat. He won a Grammy for the star-studded album *The Healer* in 1989. Hooker continued recording into the 1990s and collaborating with rock artists.

Howlin' Wolf
(Guitar, vocals, 1910–76)

Howlin' Wolf was born Chester Burnett in West Point, Mississippi, and learned the blues from Charley Patton and harmonica from Sonny Boy Williamson, who married his half-sister. After the Army, he began performing around West Memphis, Arkansas, wowing fans with his aggressive vocals and newfangled electric guitar. Promoting himself on local radio, he was heard by Sam Phillips, who cut Wolf's first sides at Phillips' Memphis Recording Service. Phillips leased the results to Chess, and Wolf was on his way.

For Chess, Wolf had hits with 'Evil' and 'Smokestack Lightnin''. But his career headed to a new level in 1960, when he was teamed with writer Willie Dixon. The combination produced a spate of mid-1960s hits, including 'I Ain't Superstitious', 'Back Door Man', 'Spoonful' and 'Wang Dang Doodle'. Wolf toured Europe and inspired The Rolling Stones, whose version of 'The Red Rooster' ('Little Red Rooster') reached No. 1 in Britain. His material was also recorded by The Doors, Cream and Jeff Beck. Later solo albums were not as successful, and in the 1970s his health began to fail. He died in a Veterans' Administration Hospital in 1976.

John Lee Hooker

Robert Johnson
(Guitar, vocals, 1911–38)

Despite recording only 29 songs in his short life, bluesman Johnson is an almost mythical figure and one of the most influential guitarists in the history of music. Born in Hazlehurst, Mississippi, in 1911, Johnson learned guitar from players like Charley Patton and Son House and supported himself on the road from the Mississippi and Arkansas deltas to the big towns of St Louis, Detroit, Chicago, and elsewhere.

Johnson's myth includes stories that he sold his soul to the devil and that he was tormented by nightmares of hellhounds until his untimely death from pneumonia after being poisoned by a jealous husband. But Johnson's true power came from an intense desire to excel and a ferocious work ethic. His first hit 'Terraplane Blues' floored listeners with its haunting vocals and guitar technique. Subsequent hits, like 'Cross Road Blues', 'Love In Vain' and 'Sweet Home Chicago', have influenced guitarists everywhere and been regularly remade by modern bands.

B.B. King
(Guitar, vocals, b. 1925)

Riley B. King, from Indianola, Mississippi, is arguably the last surviving authentic blues artist. Orphaned, he took up guitar aged 15, turning professional after US military service. In 1947, he moved to Memphis and lived with cousin Bukka White. There, he worked on a local radio station, acquiring his B.B. ('Blues Boy') epithet, also working with Bobby Bland and Johnny Ace. First recording in 1949, his breakthrough came with 1951's four-week US R&B chart-topper 'Three O'Clock Blues'. R&B hits continued, but after signing with ABC-Paramount circa 1964, he regularly crossed over to the US pop singles chart, also making the US pop album chart from 1968, with big albums like *Live And Well* and *Completely Well* (both 1959), *Live In Cook County Jail* (1971) and 1974's gold-certified *Together For The First Time … Live with Bobby Bland*. King toured relentlessly, and was said to have played 300 gigs per year between the mid-1950s and the late 1970s. Widely regarded as a true legend, King still performs and records, and has frequently guested with younger blues guitarists such as Eric Clapton, even sharing a 1989 minor US hit single, 'When Love Comes To Town', with U2.

Jerry Lee Lewis
(Piano, vocals, b. 1935)

After signing to Sun Records in 1957, Louisiana-born rock'n'roller Lewis, noted for his percussive piano style, opened his account with two million-selling US Top 3 hits, 'Whole Lotta Shakin' Going On' and 'Great Balls Of Fire' (both 1957), but caused major media controversy during a 1958 UK tour when it was discovered that his wife, who was also his cousin, was 13 years old (legal in parts of the US, unacceptable in the UK). This blighted his pop career, but from the late 1960s onwards, he combined the rockabilly that made him famous with country music, becoming a major US star with over 60 US country hits, many making the Top 10, including his chart-topping 1972 revival of 'Chantilly Lace'. Now over 70, Lewis continues to tour, and remains one of the greatest early rock'n'rollers. Dennis Quaid played him in 1989's *Great Balls Of Fire* movie.

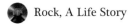

Little Richard

(Piano, vocals, b. 1932)

Georgia-born Richard Penniman, who combines frantic vocals with uninhibited pianistics, was one of 12 children. Raised in a religious family, he started recording for RCA in 1951 after winning a talent contest. Chart success followed his signing with Specialty Records, where Bumps Blackwell produced a series of classic rock'n'roll tracks between 1955 and 1958, including 1955's 'Tutti Frutti', 1956's million-selling 'Long Tall Sally' and 'Rip It Up', 1957's 'Lucille' and 'Keep A-Knockin'' and 1958's 'Good Golly Miss Molly', among others. While touring Australia in 1957, he abandoned the music business, apparently after seeing the Russian Sputnik space rocket, which he felt was a divine sign to change his behaviour. He studied to become a preacher, only recording gospel music, but returned to the fray in the mid-1960s. While he remained a dynamic live performer and an undoubted legend, his records rarely matched his 1950s rock'n'roll hits.

Little Richard

Muddy Waters

(Guitar, vocals, 1913–83)

Born McKinley Morganfield in Mississippi, Muddy Waters was first recorded by musicologist Alan Lomax. Waters' first recording for Lomax, 'I Be's Troubled', would become his first hit when he recorded it in Chicago as 'I Can't Be Satisfied' (1948). By 1951, Waters was on the R&B charts consistently with tunes like 'Louisiana Blues' and 'Long Distance Call'.

In 1952, he created the smash 'She Moves Me', and later came '(I'm Your) Hoochie Coochie Man' and 'I'm Ready'. Bo Diddley borrowed a Waters beat for 'I'm A Man' in 1955, and then Waters reworked the idea into 'Mannish Boy'. In 1956, Waters had three more R&B smashes, but as rock'n'roll developed he became a blues elder statesman to followers like The Rolling Stones (named after a Waters tune), Johnny Winter and Eric Clapton. Waters continued performing to acclaim and releasing albums to mixed results into the 1980s.

Roy Orbison

(Singer/songwriter, 1936–88)

Born in Texas, the high-voiced Orbison first recorded with Norman Petty, but his first US chart success was 1956's rockabilly 'Ooby Dooby' on Sun Records. After writing 'Claudette' (a 1957 hit for The Everly Brothers), he became a Nashville songwriter for Acuff-Rose, and restarted his recording career with 1960's million-selling ballad 'Only The Lonely', setting a pattern for many later woebegone hits, including 1961's US No. 1 'Running Scared', 1964's UK No. 1 'It's Over' and US and UK No. 1 'Oh, Pretty Woman' (1964). A 1965 label change and evolution of pop music saw his US hits end in 1967, and his UK hits in 1969, while he was beset with family tragedies. In 1988, he joined The Traveling Wilburys with George Harrison, Bob Dylan, Tom Petty and Jeff Lynne, who all held him in high esteem, but he died of a heart attack before he could take real advantage of his restored popularity.

Elvis Presley

(Singer 1935–77)

Elvis Aaron Presley was born in Tupelo, Mississippi, on 8 January 1935. He showed musical aptitude early, and sang at church. The family moved to Memphis when Elvis was 13 and he began absorbing music of all genres.

In the summer of 1953, he recorded some tracks at Sam Phillips's Sun Studio. He returned in 1954, and Sam put him together with two older musicians: guitarist Scotty Moore and bassist Bill Black.

At the session on 5 July 1954 they recorded an old Arthur Crudup blues number – 'That's All Right'. Phillips realized that this was what he had been searching for: a charismatic young white man who could combine country and blues. The single was rush-released soon after and it lit up the Memphis area. It soon became apparent that Elvis had the live act to promote the music.

Essential Recordings

1954 *That's All Right*
1955 *Mystery Train*
1956 *Heartbreak Hotel*, *Elvis*
1958 *Jailhouse Rock*
1960 *Elvis Is Back!*
1969 *In The Ghetto*, *From Elvis In Memphis*, *Suspicious Minds*
1972 *American Trilogy*
1998 *Memories: '68 Comeback Special*
1999 *Sunrise (all the Sun recordings)*

At this time Colonel Tom Parker became Presley's manager and Elvis's contract with Sun was sold to RCA in late 1955.

On 10 January 1956 Elvis, Black and Moore recorded 'Heartbreak Hotel' at RCA's Nashville Studios with Floyd Cramer and Chet Atkins on piano and guitar respectively. It became his first No. 1 and a stream of high quality rock'n'roll followed: 'I Want You, I Need You, I Love You', 'Hound Dog', 'Too Much' and 'All Shook Up' all went to US No. 1. He also made his first four movies at this time: *Love Me Tender* (1956), *Loving You* (1957), *Jailhouse Rock* (1957) and *King Creole* (1958). Elvis was drafted into the US Army in March 1958.

When Elvis was demobbed in March 1960, he guested on Frank Sinatra's ABC TV show. This was a far cry from the earlier *Ed Sullivan Show,* when cameras were ordered to cut his youth-corrupting pelvis-swivels from shot. Estimable tracks still emerged – 'A Mess Of Blues' (1960) and 'Return To Sender' (1962) – but they were outnumbered by tracks taken from the films he made, such as 'Wooden Heart' (1964) and 'Do The Clam' (1965).

Elvis was not happy with his career at this point and neither were his fans. His return to form can be traced to the June 1968 NBC TV show, the *Comeback Special,* that relaunched his career. Reunited with Scotty Moore, he performed songs from his back catalogue with a fervour he had not mustered for years. *From Elvis In Memphis* (1969) yielded 'In The Ghetto', and 'Suspicious Minds' (1969) gave him his first No. 1 for over four years.

Presley returned to regular live performance for the next couple of years but his wife Priscilla left in late 1971, and it affected Elvis badly. His drug problem increased massively, and live shows often suffered. On 16 August 1977, he died of heart failure at his Memphis home.

Elvis was the first and ultimate rock star, and played a massive part in creating the genre of rock'n'roll. He was the most charismatic performer in popular music history, and one of the most talented.

'There have been a lotta tough guys. There have been pretenders. And there have been contenders. But there is only one king.'

Bruce Springsteen

Hank Williams

T-Bone Walker

(Guitar, vocals, 1910–75)

Dallas-bred Aaron Walker was soloing on electric guitar as early as 1940, setting a trend that would eventually be the most commonplace image in rock music. B.B. King marvelled at Walker's ability to play while holding the guitar away from his body. Walker left Texas in the 1930s and alternated between sessions and performances in Los Angeles, Chicago and, later, Europe, as he advanced the instrumental appeal of blues.

Walker's peak years were the 1940s and 1950s. He found work in LA as a dancer and singer, and used both skills in his own shows when he formed his own group. Working for multiple labels like Capitol, Black & White, Imperial and Atlantic, T-Bone wowed fans with potent jams like 'Mean Old World', 'T-Bone Shuffle', 'Strollin' With Bones' and the immortal 'Stormy Monday'. Late in life Walker won a Grammy for *Good Feelin'*, a 1970 LP.

Hank Williams

(Singer/songwriter, 1923–53)

Insofar as rock has been shaped by country music, it has been shaped by Hank Williams. Williams, a superstar at 25 and dead at 29, set standards for popular as well as country music, and was a virtual hit songwriting machine. Yet, like several young rock stars who followed him, he was unable to manage stardom and drifted into alcoholism and addiction.

Williams started out performing around his native Alabama. He landed a spot on a local radio station, and was signed to MGM Records by 1947. By 1951 his songs were being covered by the biggest mainstream artists, and Hank was appearing with them on stage and television to sing hits like 'Your Cheatin' Heart', 'Cold Cold Heart', 'Jambalaya' and 'Hey, Good Lookin''. But his life and career collapsed after his divorce from his manager/wife Audrey, and he died in the back of his car in the early hours of New Year's Day, 1953.

'The thing the sixties did was to show us the possibilities and the responsibility that we all had. It wasn't the answer. It just gave us a glimpse of the possibility.'

John Lennon

The Sixties

The Sixties: ROCK GETS INTO THE SWING OF IT!

It was the decade that began with a whimper and ended with a bang. The 1960s saw rock not only come of age but also become the pre-eminent cultural force, peaking in an explosion of energy, colour and creativity that has never been equalled since.

Stateside Influence

Throughout the 1960s a number of scenes co-existed around the world, all of which would feed into each other to create a 'big bang' effect in youth culture. In Southern California, the surf craze owed its soundtrack to Dick Dale, Jan and Dean and, most importantly, The Beach Boys, while the dingy clubs of London saw young bands such as The Rolling Stones, The Pretty Things and The Yardbirds all heavily influenced by the primal beat and sexually explicit lyrics of old blues masters such as Bo Diddley, Muddy Waters and Howlin' Wolf.

Essential Recordings

- **1964** The Beatles: *A Hard Day's Night*
- **1965** Bob Dylan: *Highway 61 Revisited*
- **1966** The Beach Boys: *Pet Sounds*
- **1967** Jimi Hendrix: *Are You Experienced?*

From The Soul

The decade also saw the birth of soul music, a mixture of gospel and rhythm & blues that had begun to emerge in the late 1950s. Solomon Burke's first recordings for New York's Atlantic Records perfected the soul sound in the wake of pioneers like James Brown, Ray Charles and Sam Cooke; Stax Records issued hit records by Otis Redding, Wilson Pickett and Booker T. and The M.G.s – though they were later rivalled by a run of fabulous singles by the Queen of Soul, Aretha Franklin, for Atlantic; and Tamla Motown created worldwide hits for the likes of The Supremes, Four Tops, Martha and The Vandellas, Marvin Gaye and The Temptations. Another name, Stevie Wonder, would mature from teen sensation to mature genius over the years to come.

The Fab Four

But there was one band and one city in particular that that stamped their mark indelibly on the world at large and fired the public imagination – four lads from Liverpool by the name of The Beatles. Over the course of the decade The Fab Four, as they were christened by an eager press, created a catalogue that remains unrivalled today, their tunes still discussed in detail by serious music critics. Their home town of Liverpool and the club that launched them, the Cavern, momentarily became the epicentre of the pop world. Fellow Liverpool acts such as The Searchers, Gerry and The Pacemakers and The Swinging Blue Jeans led the way, and most of the big cities in the UK would be similarly rocked by the ensuing beat boom.

The Mods And The Rockers

Black music was popular with an emergent youth cult in Britain known as the mods, a rebellious group of young men and women who favoured the latest fashions from the Carnaby Street and Swinging London scenes, amphetamines and motor scooters (as opposed to their arch-rivals the rockers, whose predilection was for old-style leather jackets and motorbikes). Out of mod culture would emerge some of the greatest English rock bands of all time, notably The Who, Small Faces and The Kinks.

The Beat Goes On

Many talented singer/songwriters came out of the coffee houses and folk clubs along Bleeker Street in the fertile bohemian area of New York City – but all were overshadowed by the 1960s' greatest spokesman, Bob Dylan. Many young American kids began picking up on both Dylan's articulate, very relevant songs and the punchy beat of the British invaders. The Byrds' first single released in early summer of 1965, a version of Dylan's 'Mr Tambourine Man', started off the folk rock phenomenon.

Far Out

The all-out revolution in American popular music that followed not only drew on different traditional forms, but was also inspired by the prevailing political climate such as the escalating war in Vietnam and by the advent of a new 'wonder drug', LSD, which caught on amongst young kids in San Francisco smitten with the folk rock boom. Bands like Jefferson Airplane took folk rock on to its next stage, bringing folk, blues and elements of pop together with the kind of improvisational ability enjoyed by jazz players such as John Coltrane and Miles Davis.

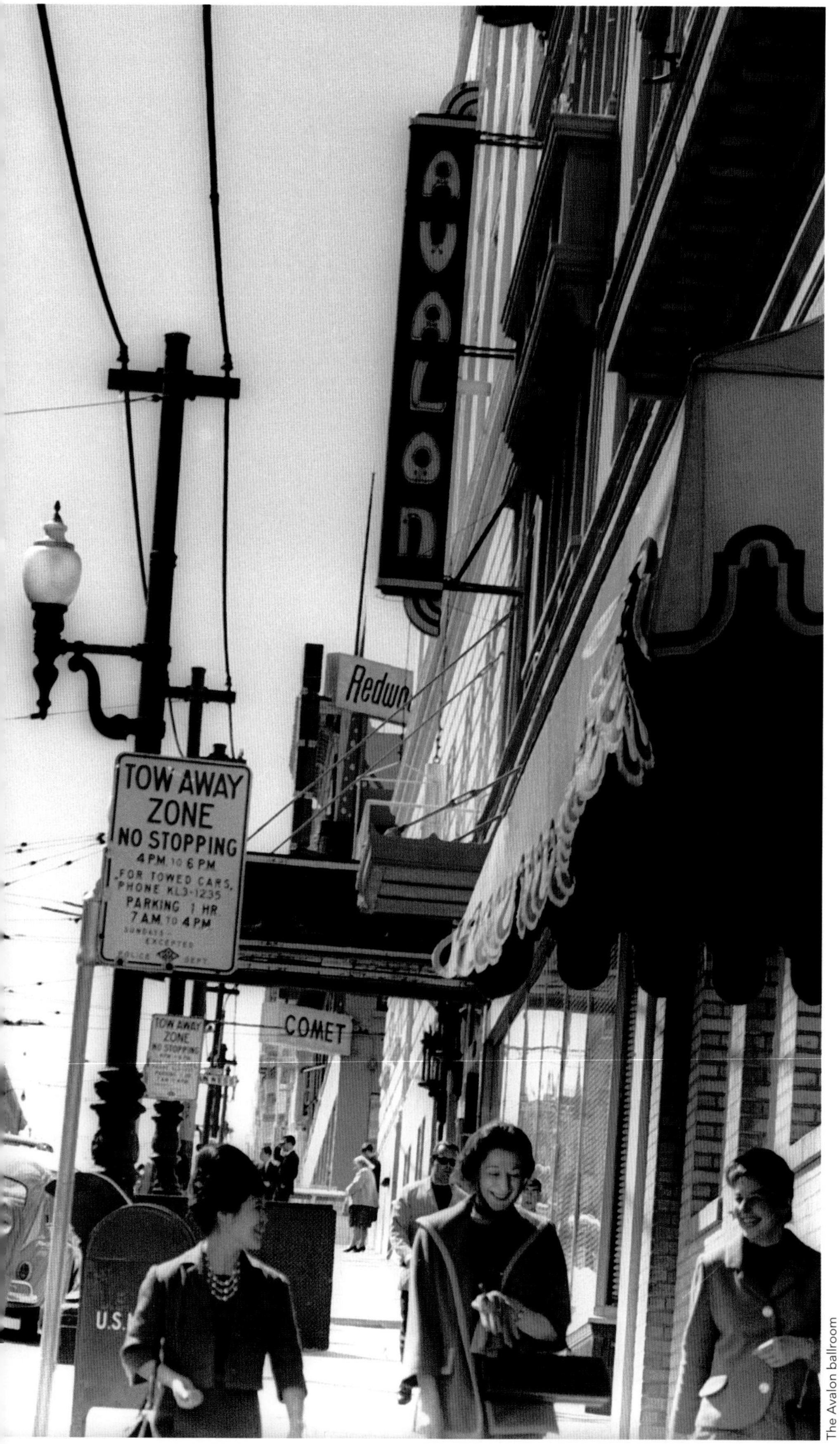

The Avalon ballroom

The Summer Of Love

By 1967, the San Francisco sound had become the backdrop to the Summer of Love. Kids across the planet rejected their parents' values and joined together to grow their hair long and espouse brotherly love. The hippie movement had arrived.

Indeed, by the middle of the decade rock was developing at a rate never witnessed before or since. Dylan went electric, alienating some of his more traditional fans, while The Beatles quit touring and concentrated on composition and working in the studio, capturing the *zeitgeist* with *Sgt. Pepper's Lonely Hearts Club Band* (1967). The same year saw Lou Reed's Velvet Underground cut their own eponymous art rock masterpiece in New York under the aegis of Pop Art guru Andy Warhol.

An Electric Revolution

A revolution in electric guitar-playing was kick-started by the arrival in London in autumn 1966 of a young black musician, Jimi Hendrix, who took the sound of blues guitar out of the Mississippi delta and launched it into space. During the few short years he was alive, Hendrix became one of the most influential figures in rock.

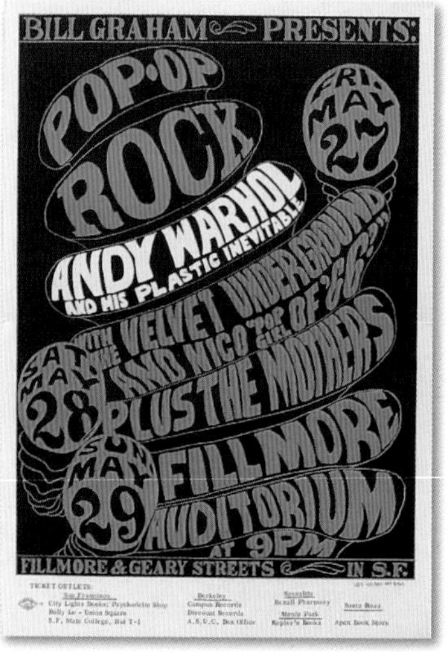

New types of club sprang up to cater for the new music and the new audience: elaborate environments such as the Avalon and Fillmore ballrooms in the US and places like the UFO club in London. One feature of these venues never before witnessed was the advent of the light show.

One band that pioneered the mixed-media concept and took rock off in yet another direction was Cambridge's Pink Floyd, whose forte was long spacey numbers like 'Interstellar Overdrive'. Rock began to look to the avant-garde for inspiration, and bands like Soft Machine, Frank Zappa's Mothers Of Invention and Captain Beefheart and His Magic Band became the order of the day.

New Vibrations

Rock as a cultural phenomenon was now separating from 'pop'. Bands were now, for the most part, writing their own material. The 45-rpm single was no longer perceived as the most important medium by which to reach

the public – the long-playing (LP) album now held sway – and the sleeves in which records were clothed became almost as important as the music itself (think Rick Griffin's mind-blowing artwork for The Grateful Dead or Martin Sharpe's day-glo designs for Cream).

The End Of The Love-In?

The late 1960s saw live music events grow in size as hundreds of thousands of fans got together in tribal gatherings: the Human Be-In in San Francisco and Monterey Pop further down the coast. There were the big Isle of Wight Festivals, free concerts in Hyde Park and, biggest of all, the Woodstock Festival in upstate New York in the summer of 1969. Yet despite all the optimism, the 1960s ended on a sour note with The Beatles in disarray, a disillusioned Dylan making a country & western album, and a death at the Altamont Festival when Hell's Angels security guards clashed with an audience member.

After the excesses of psychedelia came a return to roots by musicians on both sides of the Atlantic. The 1960s had been a decade that had achieved so much but, as the 1970s dawned, excess, disillusionment and death replaced the celebration of life and its vibrant spirit. The pendulum was swinging once again....

'Back in those days, all us skinny white British kids were trying to look cool and sound black. And there was Hendrix, the ultimate in black cool. Everything he did was natural and perfect.'

Ronnie Wood, The Rolling Stones

Headline Acts

The Animals

(Vocal/instrumental group, 1962–66, 1975–76, 1983)

After million-selling 'House Of The Rising Sun' in 1964, Tyneside's Eric Burdon (vocals), Hilton Valentine (guitar), Alan Price (keyboards), Chas Chandler (bass) and John Steel (drums) racked up further international smashes and, by 1965, music press popularity polls had them breathing down the necks of The Beatles and The Rolling Stones. Price then left to pursue a solo career and was replaced by Dave Rowberry from The Mike Cotton Sound. It was business as usual for The Animals until they disbanded after 1966's 'Don't Bring Me Down' fell from the Top 20. Burdon was persuaded to front a New Animals, who racked up hits of a psychedelic tinge. The old line-up reassembled for periodic reunion concerts and for two albums – 1976's *Before We Were So Rudely Interrupted* and, more notably, *Ark* in 1983, which they promoted – along with a re-released 'House Of The Rising Sun' – on a world tour.

The Band

(Vocal/instrumental group, 1964–76)

1968's *Music From Big Pink* was, like most subsequent Band albums, a true blend of electric folklore nurtured over rough nights in Canadian palais with rock'n'roller Ronnie Hawkins before Robbie Robertson (guitar), Richard Manuel (piano, vocals), Rick Danko (bass), Garth Hudson (organ, saxophone) and Levon Helm (drums) landed a job backing Bob Dylan, who would be in an all-star cast at *The Last Waltz*, a 1976 concert film that marked The Band's farewell to the road.

The Animals

The Beatles

The Beatles

(Vocal/instrumental group, 1960–70)

Consisting of John Lennon, Paul McCartney, George Harrison and Ringo Starr, The Beatles are the most successful, acclaimed and influential act in the history of popular music.

Born and raised in Liverpool, the soon-to-be Fab Four became a local phenomenon at the end of 1960. One of their favoured venues – and the one with which they would for ever be associated – was the Cavern Club. This is where they met Brian Epstein in 1961. He witnessed one of the group's energetic if undisciplined performances - clad in tight-fitting leather outfits and now sporting unusual 'moptop' hairdos, they went their own route ... until Epstein became their manager.

In 1962, the major labels still were not interested in groups from north of the nation's capital and they all ignored Epstein's assertion that 'One day these boys will be bigger than Elvis' ... save for the last one he approached, EMI's small Parlophone label, run by George Martin. Intrigued as much by their captivating personalities as by their musical ability, Martin signed The Beatles and both parties would never look back. Beatlemania was about to begin!

During the next seven years, the Fab Four scaled heights that were unprecedented even by Elvis Presley's standards; critically, commercially and, most enduring of all, artistically. Since the early days of their collaboration, Lennon and McCartney had written songs both separately and together, and while few of these had surpassed the standard of the group's workmanlike first single, 'Love Me Do', once they had a record company consistently demanding new material the pair went into another gear, producing songs of incredible range and increasing sophistication. From the infectious early likes of 'Please Please Me' and 'She Loves You', through to hits such as 'A Hard Day's Night', 'Can't Buy Me Love' and 'I Feel Fine', their compositions saw them slay America and the rest of the world.

As Beatlemania ran its course and the group members became jaded with the trappings of fame and non-stop concert, TV and radio appearances, they quit the road, withdrew to the EMI Studios on Abbey Road and embarked on the second and artistically even more remarkable phase of their career. Between 1966 and 1969, drawing on personal experiences, socio-cultural influences, Harrison's immersion in Indian music and philosophy, and Lennon's prodigious ingestion of mind-bending drugs, they produced recordings of breathtaking scope. From the albums *Revolver* (1966), *Sgt. Pepper's Lonely Hearts Club Band* (1967), *The Beatles* (a.k.a. *The White Album*, 1968) and *Abbey Road* (1969) The Beatles created a vast body of work, leaving a musical legacy that, more than 40 years after the band's demise, still has a solid grip on the mass consciousness.

Essential Recordings

1963 *Please Please Me, She Loves You, I Want To Hold Your Hand, With The Beatles*
1964 *A Hard Day's Night, I Feel Fine*
1965 *Day Tripper, We Can Work It Out, Rubber Soul*
1966 *Revolver*
1967 *Penny Lane, Strawberry Fields Forever, Sgt. Pepper's Lonely Hearts Club Band, Hello Goodbye, I Am The Walrus*
1968 *Lady Madonna, The Beatles, Hey Jude*
1969 *Abbey Road*
1994–6 *Live At The BBC, Anthology 1, Anthology 2, Anthology 3*

'We don't like their sound, and guitar music is on the way out.' **Decca Recording Company rejecting The Beatles, 1962**

The Beach Boys

(Vocal group, 1961–present)

The group initially achieved fame with a line-up consisting of the Wilson brothers, Brian, Dennis and Carl, together with their cousin Mike Love and Al Jardine.

Growing up in a Los Angeles suburb, their first release, 'Surfin'' (1961) helped secure the Boys a contract with Capitol Records. However, Jardine quit the band and 15-year-old David Marks took his place. Their first album, *Surfin' Safari*, which was released in late 1962, helped ignite the surf rock craze.

As the band caught fire on first a local and then a national level, Capitol began demanding new material at a frenetic rate, with no less than four more albums by the end of 1963. Still, there were many classic tracks along the way, including 'Catch A Wave', 'Little Deuce Coupe', and the sublime harmony-laced ballads 'Surfer Girl' and 'In My Room'.

Classic Recordings

1962 *Surfin' Safari*
1963 *Surfer Girl, In My Room*
1964 *Fun, Fun, Fun, I Get Around, Don't Worry Baby*
1965 *Help Me Rhonda, California Girls*
1966 *Pet Sounds, Good Vibrations*
1967 *Heroes And Villains*
1971 *Surf's Up*

Jardine was offered a second chance when he was asked to reclaim his job from Marks, and The Beach Boys' fortunes continued through 1964 courtesy of several new albums with a string of infectious hit singles – 'Fun, Fun, Fun', chart topper 'I Get Around' and 'Dance, Dance, Dance'. The ongoing pressure to deliver was too much for Brian, he suffered a nervous breakdown and quit the road for good.

While his place was taken by multi-instrumentalist Bruce Johnston, Brian focused on his songwriting which, as illustrated by tracks like 'When I Grow Up (To Be A Man)' and the chart-topping 'Help Me, Rhonda', was moving away from sun-and-sea-drenched teen themes into far more contemplative and introspective areas. Songs such as 'Wouldn't It Be Nice' and 'God Only Knows' revealed not only the extent of Brian's talent as a writer and arranger, but also a maturity that belied his 23 years. All appeared together, along with classic cuts like 'Sloop John B', on 1966's *Pet Sounds* album.

Brian then produced one of the all-time greatest singles in the form of the chart-topping 'Good Vibrations', which he withheld from *Pet Sounds* in order to spend six months (and $50,000) perfecting its intricately assembled, multi-sectional structure.

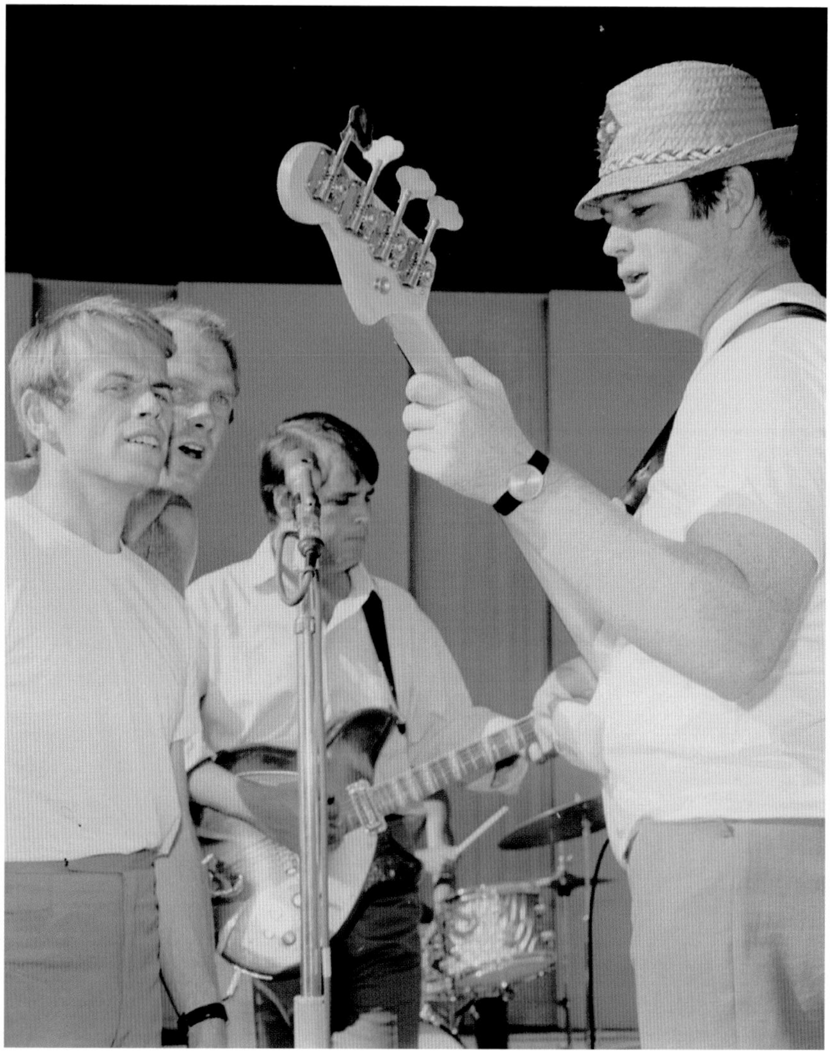

In the summer of 1966, Brian embarked on what he intended to be his avant-pop masterpiece while himself ingesting copious amounts of drugs. The musical results became as fragmented and disjointed as his own fractured vision so in May 1967, having totally lost the plot after 10 months of intense work, Brian shelved the now re-titled *SMiLE* project.

Thereafter Brian increasingly confined himself to the bedroom of his Bel Air mansion and the band often soldiered on without their chief creative force. The band's ability to influence and inspire was a thing of the past as its future lay mainly in dynamic concert performances, surviving even Dennis's drink-and-drugs problems and 1983 drowning.

'Hey, surfing's getting really big. You guys ought to write a song about it.' **Dennis Wilson to brother Brian and Mike Love, 1961**

The Beach Boys

Carl's death from brain cancer in 1998 effectively put an end to The Beach Boys, yet Love and Bruce Johnston still tour with their own band under that banner.

Booker T. And The M.G.s

(Instrumental group, 1962–71, 1973–77, 1994–present)

Stax Records' house band, Booker T. and The M.G.s also toured and recorded instrumentals in their own right. More than any other group they defined the sound of 1960s soul with their sparse, funky arrangements on hits for other Stax and Atlantic stars like Wilson Pickett, Sam and Dave, and Otis Redding. Booker T. Jones, Stax's sax and organ prodigy, formed The M.G.s (Memphis Group) with Steve Cropper (guitar), Donald 'Duck' Dunn (bass, replacing Lewis Steinberg) and Al Jackson Jr. (drums).

Their first release, 1963's 'Green Onions', was a US No. 3, eventually charting at No. 7 in the UK on its re-release in 1979. Their 1968 hit 'Soul Limbo' is the BBC's TV cricket theme. Victims of their own success, they split in 1971 because of the demand for their individual services as ace sessioneers. There have been periodic high-profile reformations: in 1992 they backed Bob Dylan at Madison Square Gardens, and in 1993 toured with Neil Young.

Booker T. and The MGs

James Brown
(Vocalist, 1933–2006)

After first success as frontman of The Famous Flames with the gospel R&B hit 'Please, Please, Please' in 1956, James Brown hit the R&B No. 1 spot with 1958's 'Try Me', becoming the man with more entries on the R&B charts than anyone else, and more on the US pop charts than anyone but Elvis.

The Flames became part of the James Brown Revue, and with The Revue's backing band, the J.B.s, Brown began to make the transition from doo-wop pop to a tougher R&B sound. 1962's *Live At The Apollo* went to No. 2 in the US charts, an unprecedented crossover for an R&B act, selling over a million copies. The 1964 LP *Out Of Sight*, with its title track of jazz organ and brass groove with choppy guitar, was another R&B No. 1. With it, James Brown invented funk.

Reinvigorated by a new recording contract in 1965 and a revised J.B.s line-up, his next single 'Papa's Got A Brand New Bag' was a worldwide hit, earning Brown his first Grammy. The follow-up 'I Got You (I Feel Good)' cemented the deal, reaching No. 3 and laying the foundation for frequent US pop listings and almost uninterrupted presence in the R&B charts to 1970.

By 1975, Brown was running out of steam and a new wave of funk was lapping at his heels, led by George Clinton, Kool and The Gang and others. He was also facing financial and personal difficulties. A cameo role in the 1980 film *The Blues Brothers*, however, returned him to mainstream attention, triggering a re-evaluation of his career and a revival of the epithet 'the godfather of soul'.

But just when his fortunes were being revived his personal life disintegrated again, and 1988 saw him sentenced to six years in prison for drugs and assault. When he emerged on parole two years later, it was to a hip-hop world, in which his back catalogue was the primary source for a new generation of funk-hungry DJs looking for a good groove to sample. No longer an innovator himself, he continued to inspire others with his energetic performances up until his death.

The Byrds
(Vocal group, 1964–73, 1989–91, 2000)

The Beatles publicly proclaimed The Byrds to be their favourite American band, while Bob Dylan not only endorsed their covers of his material but actually followed their lead into folk rock.

Formed in LA in 1964 and undergoing multiple line-up changes they eventually settled with Jim McGuinn, David Crosby, Gene Clark, Chris Hillman and Michael Clarke.

Their breakthrough track, which was a shortened version of Bob Dylan's 'Mr Tambourine Man', was quickly followed by another similarly revamped Dylan cover, 'All I Really Want To Do', both featured on their stunning debut album *Mr Tambourine Man (1965)*. Also included on the album are classics such as Clark's 'I'll Feel A Whole Lot Better' and their version of Pete Seeger's 'The Bells Of Rhymney'.

The April 1966 single 'Eight Miles High' heralded in the era of psychedelic rock, although co-composer Clark quit the band shortly thereafter due to his fear of flying and the others' resentment of the extra income that his songwriting was earning him. 'Eight Miles High' was banned by many radio stations for its alleged drug references and turned out to be The Byrds' last Top 20 US single, even though they continued to enjoy success as a quartet with the innovative *Fifth Dimension* (1966) and *Younger Than Yesterday* (1967) albums.

1967 was the year that Jim turned into Roger McGuinn, after an Indonesian guru asserted that a new name would vibrate better with the universe. Apparently it did not vibrate better with either Crosby or Clarke, both of whom departed the band due to musical and personal differences, leaving McGuinn and Hillman to pick up the pieces with a variety of new musicians. These included Gram Parsons, who was on hand to record one of the first major country rock albums, *Sweetheart Of The Rodeo,* in 1968. However, this signalled the end of the classic Byrds' sound, and by 1973, following a one-album reunion of the original quintet, the end of the band itself.

Leonard Cohen

(Guitar, singer/songwriter, b. 1934)

Despite a humble vocal endowment, this acclaimed Canadian poet and novelist moved to the States in his mid-30s to make his first essay as a recording artist with 1968's sparsely arranged and all-acoustic *Songs Of Leonard Cohen*, which included the much-covered 'Bird On A Wire'. Reaching out to self-doubting adolescent diarists, it and its successors – notably *Songs From A Room* and 1971's *Songs Of Love And Hate* – were big hits, albeit much less so in North America than Europe, where he was a surprise hit at 1970's Isle of Wight festival, although the gloomy content of many of his compositions had Cohen stereotyped by the media as a merchant of melancholy. After weathering punk, in which his wordy gentility had no place, later albums such as *I'm Your Man* (1988) and *Ten New Songs* (2003) brought him to a new young audience interested in pop of far more depth than the usual.

Leonard Cohen

Cream

(Vocal/instrumental group, 1966–68, 1993, 2005)

The first and arguably most famous of hard rock's much-touted 'supergroups', Cream comprised Eric Clapton on guitar/vocals, Jack Bruce on bass/harmonica/keyboards/vocals and Ginger Baker on drums – a trio who achieved lasting fame courtesy of their technically virtuosic, jam-and-solo-laden concerts and four psychedelia-fuelled blues rock albums during the space of less than two and a half years.

Signed to Robert Stigwood's Reaction Records, the trio's debut album *Fresh Cream* (1966) made the UK Top 10 following its release that December. Clapton's superb blues guitar was perfectly complemented by Bruce's powerful vocals and inventive playing of both the bass and harmonica, while Baker jumped to the fore on his self-penned 'Toad'.

Bruce penned half of the songs on *Fresh Cream*, and he repeated the feat on 1967's *Disraeli Gears,* while Clapton was credited as a co-writer on three of the album's most famous tracks: 'Strange Brew', 'Tales Of Brave Ulysses' and 'Sunshine Of Your Love', the group's first Stateside hit single. The album was released shortly after Cream's concerts at Bill Graham's Fillmore Auditorium in San Francisco had set the pattern for them performing extended live versions of their studio recordings.

The process continued with the altogether more patchy *Wheels Of Fire* (1968), a studio-and-stage two-album set that contained both the band's worst excesses and some of its finest moments, not least Jack Bruce's superb 'White Room' and the covers of Robert Johnson's 'Crossroads' and Albert King's 'Born Under A Bad Sign'. However, while the record topped the US charts and the group was established as one of the world's top live attractions, the group members shocked everybody by deciding to call it a day. The posthumous *Goodbye* album, featuring the classic Clapton/George Harrison composition 'Badge', served as a suitable epitaph upon its release in January 1969.

Creedence Clearwater Revival

Creedence Clearwater Revival

(Vocal/instrumental group, 1967–72)

If John Fogerty (vocals, guitar), Tom Fogerty (guitar), Stuart Cook (bass) and Doug Clifford (drums) were Californian hippy in appearance, their music harked back to the energy and stylistic cliches of 1950s rock'n'roll, and their spiritual home seemed to be the swamplands of the Deep South, as instanced in titles like 'Born On The Bayou'. After 1969's 'Proud Mary' all but topped the US chart, they reached a global audience too with 'Bad Moon Rising' at No. 1 in Australia and Britain, and comparable figures for the likes of 'Green River', 'Down On The Corner', 'Travelin' Band', 'Up Around The Bend' and attendant albums that met favour with heavy rock and mainstream pop fans alike. The winning streak came to an end in 1972. Following disbandment, chief among composer John Fogerty's solo hits was 1975's 'Rockin' All Over The World' – adopted as a signature tune by Status Quo.

Crosby, Stills And Nash

(Vocal/instrumental group, 1968–70)

When on a US tour with The Hollies, Graham Nash (vocals, guitar) had sown the seeds of a 'supergroup' with ex-Byrd Dave Crosby (vocals, guitar) and Steve Stills (vocals, guitar) from Buffalo Springfield. The new combine rehearsed in London for an eponymous album that featured hippy lyricism, flawless vocal harmonies and neo-acoustic backing tracks. Its spin-off single, Nash's 'Marrakesh Express', was a worldwide smash, and, if his trio's warblings were not to everyone's taste, they were well-received at Woodstock – only their second stage appearance – where they were joined by Neil Young, a Buffalo Springfield colleague of Stills, who stayed on for 1970's *Deja Vu*, attributed to Crosby, Stills, Nash and Young. The group broke up the following year to devote themselves principally to solo careers, though the four individuals reunited for Live Aid and a 1988 album, *American Dream*.

Rogers
ave Clark

The Dave Clark Five

(Vocal/instrumental group, 1958–70)

Prior to the issue of an instrumental single, 'Chaquita', in 1962, this London combo underwent fundamental personnel reshuffles, resulting in a line-up that remained stable for the rest of its career. Then Dave Clark (drums), Lenny Davidson (guitar), Denis Payton (saxophone), Rick Huxley (bass) and Mike Smith (vocals, keyboards) switched their stylistic emphasis to music with vocals. After a 1964 chart topper, 'Glad All Over', and its 'Bits And Pieces' follow-up – both written by Smith and Clark – the group racked up heftier achievements in the States as a foremost 'British invasion' act. Their only major film, *Having A Wild Weekend* (UK title: *Catch Us If You Can*) was a box-office triumph, and – also in 1965 – 'Over And Over' was a US No. 1, but many later releases were characterized by bandwagon-jumping. Clark's main public activities since have been 1970s recordings with Smith as 'Dave Clark And Friends', promoting repackagings of The Five's hits, and 1987's *Time* musical, praised mostly for its spectacular visual effects.

Donovan

Donovan

(Guitar, vocals, b. 1946)

After 'Catch The Wind' and 'Colours' charted in 1965, this projected English 'answer' to Bob Dylan lost impetus until he mined a seam of 'sunshine' pop with songs such as 'Sunshine Superman' – a US No. 1 – and 'Jennifer Juniper'. After 'Atlantis' foundered in 1968's UK Top 30, he bounced back briefly with 'Goo Goo Barabajagal (Love Is Hot)', a liaison with The Jeff Beck Group. Since then, only a 1990 comedy revival of 'Jennifer Juniper' (with Singing Corner) has been even a minor hit.

The Doors

(Vocal/instrumental group, 1965–73, 1978, 1993, 1997, 2000, 2011)

Jim Morrison (vocals) has been the posthumous subject of a movie that fuelled the myth that he *was* The Doors. If his stage antics brought the Los Angeles outfit much publicity – and notoriety – their hits were either team efforts or written by other personnel, namely Ray Manzarek (keyboards), Robbie Kreiger (guitar) and John Densmore (drums). 1967's 'Light My Fire', a US No. 1, was followed by further high placings in both the single and album lists, peaking in 1968 with million-sellers 'Hello I Love You' and 'Touch Me'. Then came a concert in Miami where Morrison was purported to have exposed himself. During a long wait for the scheduled trial, he exiled himself in Paris, where he died suddenly in 1971. The Doors disbanded two years later after two albums without him – though they reconvened in 1978 to provide accompaniment on *An American Prayer*, an album centred on tapes of Morrison reciting self-written poems. Since then, action has deferred to debate concerning a more permanent reformation with a new lead singer.

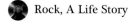

Bob Dylan

(Guitar, singer/songwriter, b. 1941)

Next to The Beatles, Bob Dylan was the most influential artist of his generation. While cross-pollinating folk and country with electric rock, Dylan elevated the role of the singer/songwriter and, in so doing, introduced an entirely new dimension to popular music.

His eponymous first album (1962) was mainly an assortment of folk, blues and gospel covers. However, it was a totally different story by the time *The Freewheelin' Bob Dylan* was released in May 1963, a cover of 'Corrina, Corrina' standing alone amid a dozen self-penned tracks. Given the political climate of the times, the last two songs attracted the most attention: 'A Hard Rain's A-Gonna Fall', conjuring brutal images of nuclear Armageddon, and 'Blowin' In The Wind', with its heartfelt call for change.

Essential Recordings

1963 *The Freewheelin' Bob Dylan*
1964 *The Times They Are A-Changin'*, *Another Side Of Bob Dylan*
1965 *Bringing It All Back Home*, *Highway 61 Revisited*
1966 *Blonde On Blonde*
1967 *John Wesley Harding*
1969 *Nashville Skyline*
1970 *New Morning*
1975 *Blood On The Tracks*, *The Basement Tapes*
1976 *Desire*
1997 *Time Out Of Mind*
2001 *Love And Theft*
2009 *Together Through Life*

The January 1964 release of *The Times They Are A-Changin'* continued the cycle of protest songs, its outstanding title track sounding a warning to parents and politicians about the crumbling status quo, yet just eight months later *Another Side Of Bob Dylan* proved to be just that: partly more romantic, invariably more poetic, with greater depth and imagery to both the music and the lyrics.

Shocking and enraging the folk world by going 'electric' on *Bringing It All Back Home* (1965), Dylan was projected into the pop mainstream.

He then secured a massive worldwide audience with his breakthrough single 'Like a Rolling Stone' which, at just over six minutes, was roughly twice the length of conventional releases. Dylan was redefining the parameters of popular music.

The music of *Highway 61 Revisited* (1965) veered between the blues of 'It Takes A Lot To Laugh, It Takes A Train To Cry' and the all-out rock of the title track and 'Tombstone Blues'. Lyrically, Dylan was now a streetwise beat poet, and this was an image that he would stick with, reaching its apotheosis on arguably his finest record, the double album *Blonde On Blonde* (1966).

On 29 July 1966, just over two months after *Blonde On Blonde*'s release, Dylan suffered a near-fatal motorcycle accident and thereafter he was a changed man. Following several months of recording demos with The Hawks (later The Band), the *John Wesley Harding* (1967) and *Nashville Skyline* (1969) albums signalled Dylan's foray into the much calmer waters of country rock.

Although 1970's *Self Portrait* incited the first uniformly critical drubbing of Dylan's career, the new decade saw him sustain a fairly high degree of success with his albums between 1970–79.

Since 1988, Dylan has fronted what has come to be known as his 'Never Ending Tour' of the globe, while returning to form in the studio. *Together Through Life*, his first studio album since 2006, hit the top slot on both sides of the Atlantic in 2009, making him the oldest living person to go straight into the chart at No. 1. He remains one of the world's most formidable and relevant artists.

'If Woody Guthrie set the bar for American songwriters, Bob Dylan jumped right over it.'

John Mellencamp

Fleetwood Mac

Fairport Convention

(Vocal/instrumental group, 1967–79, 1985–present)

Not so much a premier folk rock ensemble as one of the most English of veteran rock bands, Fairport formed in London in 1967 in a vague image of Jefferson Airplane, but traditional folk pervaded a second LP, *What We Did On Our Holidays* (1969), on which singer Sandy Denny debuted, and those that followed. Representatives of all line-ups have pitched in at Cropredy, the annual festival over which the group have presided since the early 1980s.

Fleetwood Mac

(Vocal/instrumental group, 1967–95, 1997–present)

Peter Green (vocals, guitar) had been a star of John Mayall's Bluesbreakers, in which John McVie (bass) and Mick Fleetwood (drums) had toiled less visibly. In 1967, the three became 'Peter Green's Fleetwood Mac' after enlisting guitarist Jeremy Spencer. Later, a third guitarist, Danny Kirwan, was added. The outfit produced hits like 'Albatross' and 'Oh Well'. Green's exit in 1970 brought the group to its knees but acted as a catalyst for the birth of a new sound from the band.

The Four Seasons
(Vocal group, 1960–present)

In 1962, after performing as The Four Lovers, New Jersey session singers Frankie Valli, Tommy DeVito and Nick Massi plus songwriter Bob Gaudio issued a single, 'Sherry', as The Four Seasons. With Valli's shrill falsetto to the fore, it was an international million-seller. Other such triumphs of the same persuasion included 'Big Girls Don't Cry', 'Rag Doll' and 1965's 'Let's Hang On'. By 1968, the momentum had slackened, but the group enjoyed a further brace of chartbusters during the late 1970s disco boom.

Four Tops
(Vocal group, 1953–present)

The Detroiters line-up (Levi Stubbs, Lawrence Payton, Renaldo Benson, Abdul Fakir) remained unchanged for 44 years. The 1960s signalled their heyday with a run of Top 10s, including No. 1s 'I Can't Help Myself (Sugar Pie, Honey Bunch)' and 'Reach Out I'll Be There'.

During the late 1960s and early 1970s their chart success waned until they again enjoyed success with their 1981 classic 'When She Was My Girl', and UK No. 7 'Loco In Acapulco' from 1988.

The Four Seasons

Aretha Franklin
(Vocals, b. 1942)

The undisputed Queen of Soul since the title was first applied to her in the late 1960s, Aretha Franklin has been hailed as the greatest soul diva of all time.

After making little impact with her music during her time at Columbia Records in the early 1960s, things came together with laserlike intensity in 1967 when she moved to Atlantic Records. The combination of Aretha Franklin with producer Jerry Wexler and the rock-solid R&B of the Muscle Shoals rhythm section lit a fuse that delivered an opening salvo of 10 Top 10 hits for the label in her first two years alone. The very first recording session resulted in the smouldering, gospel-tinged 'I Never Loved A Man (The Way I Love You)', while the hastily convened second produced one of the defining moments of popular music, her blazing take on Otis Redding's 'Respect'. It was an instant US No. 1, which broke her worldwide.

Her domination of the charts continued in the early 1970s and included what many consider to be her finest LP, the 1972 live, double gospel set *Amazing Grace*.

By the mid-1970s, however, she was beginning to lose her way and a switch of labels to Arista in 1980 had little initial impact. 1985 saw a return to form with the Eurythmics collaboration 'Sisters Are Doin' It For Themselves', and a US No. 1 with 'Freeway Of Love'. Her rousing 1986 duet with George Michael 'I Knew You Were Waiting (For Me)' was No. 1 in both countries.

With more US pop and R&B hits than any other woman Franklin's status as a soul institution is assured. In 2006 aged 64 she won her 17th Grammy before performing 'My Country 'Tis Of Thee' at Barack Obama's presidential inauguration three years later.

Billy Fury

Billy Fury
(Vocals, 1940–83)

This fated Liverpudlian was on a par with Cliff Richard as a British Elvis Presley, enjoying 11 Top 10 hits before vanishing into a cabaret nether-world. Though dogged by severe ill health, he resurfaced as a typecast rock'n'roll singer in the 1973 movie *That'll Be The Day*. As he may have wished, he died with a record in the charts – 1983's 'Devil Or Angel' – although he was unable either to begin a scheduled tour or complete *The Only One*, intended as a farewell album.

Marvin Gaye
(Vocals, 1939–84)

Gaye was a soul giant whose career spanned his genre's transition from pop entertainment to social conscience and personal exploration. He signed with Berry Gordy's Motown label in 1961, where his recordings revealed a strong tenor voice with a huge span – three octaves – on songs ranging from R&B mod anthem 'Can I Get A Witness' to the soulful heartache of 'I Heard It Through The Grapevine'.

He charted with duets too, notably alongside Tammi Terrell. Gaye grieved for a year after Terrell's tragic death, emerging to negotiate artistic control of his work and release 1971's *What's Going On*, routinely regarded as the greatest soul album ever, taking a radical, mature new direction addressing political and social issues. Its follow-up *Let's Get It On* (1973) dealt equally powerfully with more intimate concerns.

Although his creative light never dimmed, his later life was blighted by tax issues, failed marriages, drug dependency and depression. In 1984, his father shot him dead during a family argument.

The Grateful Dead

(Vocal/instrumental group, 1965–95)

The Grateful Dead grew out of a union between singer/songwriter/lead guitarist Jerry Garcia, songwriter/rhythm guitarist Bob Weir, Phil Lesh (bass), Bill Kreutzmann (drums) and keyboardist/singer Ron 'Pigpen' McKernan.

In March 1967 they released their eponymous debut album but it failed to reproduce the range and excitement of their live performances. *Anthem Of The Sun* (1968) went a considerable way towards correcting that problem, thanks in large part to the addition of a rock-solid second drummer, Mickey Hart, and avant-garde second keyboard player Tom Constanten. It wasn't until the in-concert double-album *Live/Dead* was released later that year that record buyers finally got to hear what the group was truly all about.

Jerry Garcia of The Grateful Dead

Back in the studio, the band recorded two classic albums in 1970 that represented a drastic change of pace and direction, contrasting sharply with its onstage act. Both the all-acoustic *Workingman's Dead* and the seminal *American Beauty* saw the Dead exploring their country, folk and blues roots in superb and remarkably restrained fashion.

Indeed, the live work would gather momentum with each passing year, as the Deadheads kept increasing in numbers, along with their use of drugs at the group's shows.

When McKernan died of liver failure Keith Godchaux replaced him, while his wife Donna Jean was recruited to sing backing vocals prior to 1973's *Wake Of The Flood*, 1974's *Grateful Dead From The Mars Hotel* and 1975's *Blues For Allah* albums, all released on the band's own label and their last good records for more than a decade. Keyboardist Brent Mydland replaced the Godchauxes in 1979.

1987's *In The Dark* spawned their only ever Top 10 single, 'Touch Of Gray'. At this point, The Dead's cult popularity went mainstream and already massive ticket sales went through the roof; yet this ongoing success was time-limited. Following Mydland's death his place was taken by ex-Tube Vince Welnick, as well as by part-time member Bruce Hornsby, and the band continued performing to sell-out crowds until Garcia's death in 1995.

Jimi Hendrix

(Vocal/guitar, 1942-70)

With his pioneering use of fuzz, feedback and distortion in tandem with a God-given talent, Jimi Hendrix expanded and redefined the range of the electric guitar, and in so doing he became one of rock's greatest superstars.

The American left-handed guitarist started his career as a session guitarist but in 1966 he moved to London and The Jimi Hendrix Experience, with guitarist Noel Redding on bass and Mitch Mitchell on drums, was formed. Within weeks, the trio's performances were creating a major buzz on the London scene, hitting the UK Top 10 three times during the first half of 1967 with the singles 'Hey Joe', 'Purple Haze' and 'The Wind Cries Mary' all of which were included on Hendrix's outstanding debut album *Are You Experienced?* (1967).

Onstage the innately shy Hendrix ignited audiences with his breathtaking musicianship and willingness to put on a show, while in the studio engineer Eddie Kramer helped realize Jimi's sonic vision by pushing the technological envelope to its absolute limits, as evidenced on *Axis: Bold As Love* (1967)

and the double album *Electric Ladyland* (1968). Hereafter, the last two years of Jimi's life would be characterized by personal and professional unrest. He folded The Experience in June 1969 and formed the funkier Band Of Gypsies with Billy Cox on bass and Buddy Miles on drums.

The Jimi Hendrix Experience was briefly reformed in early 1970 and while work was in progress on a fourth album, tentatively titled *First Rays Of The New Rising Sun,* Hendrix's death in London on 18 September of that year would prevent its completion, yet the extant tracks and numerous other unreleased recordings would posthumously see the light of day.

Herman's Hermits
(Vocal group, 1963–present)

Peter 'Herman' Noone (vocals) had been a TV actor before the group's maiden single, 1965's 'I'm Into Something Good', was a hit both at home and in the States; 'Hermania' was manifested by high Hot 100 climbs for songs such as 'Silhouettes', 'Mrs Brown You've Got A Lovely Daughter' and 'Listen People' before a predictable decline when new sensations arrived. Turning back on the European market, they managed a few more chart strikes before Noone went solo in 1971.

The Hollies
(Vocal/instrumental group, 1962–present)

The sound of Manchester's most acclaimed beat group hinged on the jazz sensibility of Bobby Elliott (drums) and, more so, on the breathtaking chorale of Allan Clarke (vocals), Tony Hicks (guitar, vocals) and Graham Nash (vocals, guitar) who, under the pseudonym 'L. Ransford', also composed many of an unbroken series of smashes from 1963 to 1968. Yet it was a non-original, 1966's 'Look Through Any Window', that broke The Hollies in the US. Though reliant more on outside writers after Nash

Herman's Hermits

The Jackson Five

left to form the Crosby, Stills and Nash 'supergroup', the run of hits continued up to 1974's 'The Air That I Breathe', and, as late as 1983, 'Stop In The Name Of Love' swept into the US Top 20. Moreover, via its use in a TV commercial, a re-release of 1969's 'He Ain't Heavy (He's My Brother)' was a domestic No. 1 in 1988. Clarke retired, but Hicks and Elliott soldiered on into the new millennium.

The Jackson Five/The Jacksons

(Vocal/instrumental group, 1964–90, 2001, 2012–present)

The last great Motown pop group, the brothers Jackson – Jackie, Tito, Marlon, Jermaine and Michael – signed in 1968 and were groomed for a year before their debut single 'I Want You Back' shot to US No. 1, followed by four more chart toppers in a row including 'ABC' and 'I'll Be There'. The huge teen following for their bubblegum soul led Motown to restrict their growth as songwriters and musicians. Frustrated, the group switched labels in 1975, changing their name because Motown retained rights to the original.

With producers Gamble and Huff they found a new maturity of sound, moving through Philly Soul ('Show You The Way To Go') to self-penned funk ('Blame It On The Boogie'), and climaxing in the masterful 1980 LP *Triumph*. Michael's emerging solo career began to overshadow the family band's (although he still contributed to Jacksons' albums) and they formally disbanded in 1990.

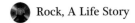

Jefferson Airplane

(Vocal/instrumental group, 1965–72, 1989, 1996)

When the 'classic' line-up of Marty Balin (vocals), Grace Slick (vocals), Paul Kantner (guitar, vocals), Jorma Kaukonen (guitar, vocals) and Skip Spence (drums) found each other, a merger of an oblique form of folk rock with psychedelia ensured acceptance by their native San Francisco's hippy community. They produced 1967 hit singles in 'Somebody To Love' and 'White Rabbit', and albums that were still charting when the group evolved into Jefferson Starship to enjoy another golden age in the 1980s.

Tom Jones

Jethro Tull

(Vocal/instrumental group, 1967–present)

While this group – originally Ian Anderson (vocals, flute), Mick Abrahams (guitar), Glenn Cornick (bass) and Clive Bunker (drums) – rose on the crest of the British 'blues boom' in the late 1960s, they absorbed many other musical idioms, principally via composer Anderson. The image of his matted hair, vagrant attire and antics with his flute during early TV appearances was not easily forgotten, for, as well as being a popular album act, especially after the second one, *Stand Up* (1969), sold well in North America, they were also mainstream pop stars by 1969 when 'Living In The Past' all but topped the UK chart. Such entries, however, dried up by 1971 when *Aqualung*, a 'concept' album, appeared. By the 1980s, the group had become Anderson and Martin Barre (guitar) plus backing musicians, whose living depended mostly upon US consumers' continued liking for 1987's Grammy-winning *Crest Of A Knave* and whatever other albums the financially secure Anderson chose to record.

Tom Jones

(Vocals, b. 1940)

This Welshman's piledriving but flexible baritone was first heard by the world at large on 1965's 'It's Not Unusual', a UK No. 1 that also reached the Top 10 in the States. A lean period ended with 'Green, Green Grass Of Home' at the top at home and high in the US Hot 100. Further hits stretched to the early 1970s, partly because the magnificence of his voice was able to ride roughshod over indifferent material, like 1971's 'Puppet Man'. In any case, chart entries had become mere sideshows now that he had found an apparent niche as a tuxedo-ed Las Vegas cabaret performer. Nonetheless, a return to the charts after a 10-year absence with 1987's 'The Boy From Nowhere' and a re-issued 'It's Not Unusual' brought much of the aura of a fresh sensation to teenage consumers. Suddenly hip, he had another smash in 1990 with a version of Prince's 'Kiss'; starred in a TV documentary by former Sex Pistols svengali Malcolm McLaren; and recorded with Robbie Williams, Stereophonics, Wyclef Jean and other modern chart contenders, intrigued by his unquiet journey to old age. In 2006, he received a knighthood.

Janis Joplin

(Vocals, 1943–70)

During a troubled adolescence in Texas, Joplin sang in regional clubs before a move to California, where she emerged as focal point of San Francisco's Big Brother and The Holding Company, sounding weary, cynical and knowing beyond her years. In 1968, she began

Ludwig
The
KINKS

a solo career that was triumphant and tragic – for, shortly after a drug-induced death in 1970, she topped both the US album and singles chart with, respectively, *Pearl* and 'Me And Bobby McGee'.

The Kinks

(Vocal/instrumental group, 1964–96)

One of the more popular bands of the 'British invasion' and a considerable influence on both 1970s heavy metal outfits and 1990s groups, The Kinks went through numerous line-up changes but were always led by singer/songwriter Ray Davies, while his brother Dave supplied the band's signature rock guitar sound.

'You Really Got Me' stormed its way to the top of the UK charts in 1964 and made the US Top 10. By 1965 the band had recorded a couple of so-so albums and several EPs while making non-stop concert and TV appearances. However, things ground to an untimely halt in America during the summer of that year when the group was banned from re-entering the country.

The ban would last four years, during which time they released *The Village Green Preservation Society* (1968) and the magnificent 1969 concept album *Arthur (Or The Decline And Fall Of The British Empire)*. Unfortunately, sales were modest; Pete Quaife quit the band after the failure of *Village Green* and was replaced by John Dalton, while the addition of keyboardist John Gosling following the release of *Arthur* turned The Kinks into a five-piece setup.

The 1970 album *Lola Versus The Powerman And The Money-Go-Round, Part One*, proved to be a surprise financial and critical success, spawning hit singles in the form of the satirical 'Lola' and 'Apeman'. For the next seven years, through various line-up changes, The Kinks enjoyed renewed success in America, both on the album charts with *Sleepwalker* (1977), *Misfits* (1978), *Low Budget* (1979) and the aptly titled *Give The People What They Want* (1981), and on the road, touring arenas to sellout crowds. In 1990 they were inducted into The Rock and Roll Hall of Fame.

Alexis Korner

(Guitar, vocals, 1928–84)

The late 'Godfather of British blues' emerged from London's traditional jazz scene to found Blues Incorporated in 1962. Among those passing through the ranks of this loose if inspirational amalgam were subsequent members of The Rolling Stones, Cream and Led Zeppelin. In the late 1960s, Korner too made the charts as singer with CCS, whose biggest hit, a cover of Led Zeppelin's 'Whole Lotta Love' became the theme tune to BBC television's *Top Of The Pops*.

The Kinks

Love

(Vocal/instrumental group, 1965–96, 2002–05, 2009–present)

Love's fusion of jingle-jangling folk rock, surreal lyrics and elements peculiar to themselves was at its purest on 1968's *Forever Changes*, a third album on which songwriting was shared between Bryan Maclean (vocals, guitar) and leader Arthur Lee (vocals, guitar). After decades out of the public eye, and a spell in prison, Lee was as ecstatic as his devotees to perform the entire *Forever Changes* at London's Royal Festival Hall in 2003. Arthur Lee died in 2006.

Manfred Mann

(Vocal/instrumental group, 1962–69)

This multifaceted ensemble – Paul Jones (vocals, harmonica), Mike Vickers (guitar, woodwinds), Manfred Mann (keyboards), Dave Richmond (bass) and Mike Hugg (drums) – first reached the national Top 20 with 1963's '5-4-3-2-1'. After Richmond was replaced by Tom McGuinness, there was hardly any let-up of hits, both home and overseas, including a US chart topper with 'Do Wah Diddy Diddy', despite other personnel changes. Some of the most enduring tracks were written by Bob Dylan, who considered Manfred Mann the most proficient exponents of his work. Indeed, the group scored a million-seller with his 'Mighty Quinn' after McGuinness switched to guitar and Mike D'Abo superceded Jones in 1966. All former members of the group achieved further success as recording artists, most remarkably Jones with two fast UK Top 5 penetrations; McGuinness did the same with his McGuinness-Flint unit, and Mann's progressive Earth Band enjoyed a longer run of hits in the 1970s.

John Mayall

(Multi-instrumentalist, vocals, b. 1933)

When he was a Manchester art student in the late 1940s, blues record sessions evolved into successful attempts at reproducing the sounds himself, so much so that he dared a stage debut in a city club in 1950. In the decades that followed, Mayall carved a niche of true individuality in perhaps pop's most stylized form, re-inventing it from all manner of new angles: duetting with Chicago bluesman Paul Butterfield on a 1967 British EP; with a big band on 1968's *Bare Wires* album; and without a drummer for 1969's near-acoustic *The Turning Point*. From the mid-1960s, his albums had been making inroads into the UK list, and his accompanying Bluesbreakers cradled many stars-in-waiting, among them guitar heroes Eric Clapton and Peter Green. Initially modest success in the States prompted an uprooting to California in 1968, and a preponderance of North American hirelings in the 1970s. He is still a reliable concert attraction and new albums remain worthwhile marketing exercises.

Joni Mitchell

(Guitar, vocals, b. 1943)

Fairport Convention were among several artists who had already covered her songs when this gifted Canadian soprano's debut LP, *Songs To A Seagull*, appeared in 1968. A move to California coupled with relentless touring assisted the passage of the following year's *Clouds*

into the US Top 40. However, it was not until she caught the general tenor of the post-Woodstock era that Mitchell truly left the runway with 1970's *Ladies Of The Canyon* and its spin-off hit single 'Big Yellow Taxi' – as well as a cover of its 'Woodstock' by Matthews' Southern Comfort climbing to No. 1 in Britain. *Blue* and 1974's *Court And Spark* – her first with all-amplified accompaniment – were particularly big sellers before a jazzier approach in the later 1970s was received less enthusiastically. Since then, artistic and commercial progress have been patchy and have involved ventures into other cultural areas – most conspicuously exhibitions of her paintings in the mid-1990s – and increasingly longer periods of vanishing from the public eye.

The Monkees

(Vocal/instrumental group, 1966–71, 1986–89, 1993–97, 2001–02, 2010–present)

Four amenable youths – Mike Nesmith (guitar), Peter Tork (vocals), Mickey Dolenz (drums) and Davy Jones (vocals) – were hired by a Hollywood business conglomerate to play an Anglo-American pop combo in a 1966 TV series that was to be networked worldwide. Success was instant, and an international No. 1 with 'I'm A Believer' precipitated further smashes that continued after the final programme in 1968. Decades later, re-runs of the series struck chords with both pre-teens and their nostalgic parents.

The Moody Blues

(Vocal/instrumental group, 1964–74, 1977–present)

Though 'Go Now' was a worldwide smash in 1965, later singles were much less successful for Denny Laine (vocals, guitar), Mike Pinder (keyboards), Ray Thomas, (woodwinds, percussion), Clint Warwick (bass) and Graeme Edge (drums), veterans of several beat groups from the British Midlands. With the departures of the late Warwick and Laine (later in Paul McCartney's Wings), the group were sagging on the ropes by 1967.

However, with the respective enlistments of John Lodge and Justin Hayward, they revived with 'Nights In White Satin', the hit 45 from *Days Of Future Passed* (1967), an ambitious concept LP with orchestra. Consequent albums refined a grandiose style so nebulous in scope that such diverse units as Yes, King Crimson and Roxy Music were all cited erroneously as variants of The Moody Blues prototype. Following a sabbatical for solo projects in the mid-1970s, the group reassembled for 1978's *Octave* and further albums that have tended to sell steadily if unremarkably.

Wilson Pickett

(Vocals, 1941–2006)

Pickett signed with Atlantic in 1965, where he scored an early hit with 'In The Midnight Hour'. More hits followed, many of them becoming dance band standards, including 'Mustang Sally' and 'Land Of 1000 Dances'.

The hits kept coming in the early 1970s, but when he quit Atlantic in 1972 the well dried up. He died in 2006 having made a lasting mark on Southern soul and dance music.

The Pretty Things

(Vocal/instrumental group, 1963–present)

Phil May (vocals) and ex-Rolling Stone Dick Taylor (guitar) formed this London R&B outfit in 1963. A long-haired reprobate image held instant appeal and they made the UK Top 20 with 'Don't Bring Me Down' and 'Honey I Need'. A few minor hits later, they signed off the singles chart for ever in 1966, and sales did not match critical acclaim for works such as *S.F. Sorrow* (1968) – unarguably the first 'rock opera' – and 1969's *Parachute, Rolling Stone* magazine's Album Of The Year.

Otis Redding

(Vocals, 1941–67)

Georgia's finest soul son, Otis Redding's story encapsulates the history of soul music. 'These Arms Of Mine' became Otis' first hit, climbing to No. 20 in the R&B chart in 1963.

Wilson Pickett

Otis Redding

But it was 1965's 'Mr Pitiful', that saw Redding start to make inroads into the pop charts. Many hits were self-penned, a mixture of towering soul ballads and harder-rocking R&B work-outs. In 1966, his songwriting talents matured on not one but two classic albums.

Otis Blue (1965), his response to the shooting the previous year of his idol Sam Cooke, included future soul standards 'I've Been Loving You Too Long' and 'Respect', and milestone reworkings of the Sam Cooke hit 'Shake' and The Rolling Stones' 'Satisfaction' (written by the Stones in imitation of his style).

Next came *Complete And Unbelievable* (1966), whose hits included 'Fa-Fa-Fa-Fa-Fa (Sad Song)', 'My Lover's Prayer' and the song for ever associated with Redding's impassioned, heart-wrenching soul voice, 'Try A Little Tenderness'.

Meanwhile, Otis Redding was building a formidable name as a live performer: he delivered his songs with the fervour of a gospel preacher, and he had dance moves to rival James Brown.

In early December 1967 he recorded some new material including '(Sittin' On) The Dock Of The Bay', but on 10 December Redding was killed in a plane crash.

'Dock Of The Bay' was a posthumous No. 1 in 1968, winning Best Song and Best R&B Vocal Grammys. Although soul music had lost a widely loved and respected singer, these were not merely sentimental awards. Four subsequent gold discs for CD anthologies, and a Lifetime Achievement Grammy in 1999 testify to the enduring talent and potential that was lost with his death.

The Righteous Brothers

(Vocal duo, 1962–68, 1974–2003)

Bill Medley and the late Bobby Hatfield struck gold in 1965 with 'You've Lost That Lovin' Feelin'', a simple song inflated by producer Phil Spector's trademark 'Wall of Sound'. Another year of hits in the same vein closed with Medley going solo. A reunion with Hatfield spawned a US-only smash,

1974's 'Rock And Roll Heaven'. In 1990, a re-release of 1965's 'Unchained Melody' – featured in the movie *Ghost* – topped the UK chart, and 'You've Lost That Lovin' Feelin'' made the Top 10 for the third time.

Smokey Robinson And The Miracles

(Vocal group, 1958–78)

Their 1960 hit 'Shop Around' set the gospel-and-soul tone for Motown. 'I Second That Emotion' (1967) broke the group in Britain. Robinson had already decided to leave before 1970's reissued 'Tears Of A Clown' reached No. 1. The Miracles had one more No. 1 without Robinson, 1976's 'Love Machine', before splitting in 1978.

Diana Ross And The Supremes

(Vocal group, 1961–77)

The jewels in the crown of Motown's golden years, The Supremes' sophisticated act and sound were the TV-friendly face of soul music, winning them 12 No. 1s. Many, like 'You Can't Hurry Love' and 'You Keep Me Hanging On', became pop classics.

Diana Ross' grooming for solo stardom dented the trio's infallibility. But hits continued into the 1970s with 'Stoned Love' and 'River Deep – Mountain High'. When third original Mary Wilson left in 1976 The Supremes finally folded. Ross went on to have a phenomenal solo career.

Diana Ross and The Supremes

The Rolling Stones

(Vocal/instrumental group, 1962–present)

In its classic line-up, featuring Mick Jagger, Keith Richards, Brian Jones, Bill Wyman and Charlie Watts, they first achieved success and notoriety as a loutish, parentally disapproved blues rock counterpoint to the equally contrived happy-go-lucky image of The Beatles.

It was at the Crawdaddy Club, located inside the Station Hotel in Richmond, South London in April 1963 that The Stones were checked out by Andrew Loog Oldham and subsequently signed to a management contract. Previously a publicist for Beatles' manager Brian Epstein, Oldham knew little about music but everything about promotion; they soon secured a record contract with Decca on the strength of a recommendation by George Harrison to A&R executive Dick Rowe.

Essential Recordings

- **1964** *Little Red Rooster, The Rolling Stones*
- **1965** *(I Can't Get No) Satisfaction, Get Off Of My Cloud*
- **1966** *Aftermath*
- **1967** *Between The Buttons*
- **1968** *Jumpin' Jack Flash, Beggars Banquet*
- **1969** *Honky Tonk Women, Let It Bleed*
- **1971** *Sticky Fingers*
- **1972** *Exile On Main St.*
- **1978** *Some Girls*
- **1981** *Tattoo You*
- **2005** *A Bigger Bang*

Next, while The Rolling Stones released their first two R&B-flavoured singles, a cover of Chuck Berry's 'Come On' and the Lennon/McCartney-donated 'I Wanna Be Your Man', Oldham flirted with moulding them in The Beatles' lovable, smiling, clean-cut image. Then he thought better of it and, in a masterstroke, cast them as the anti-Fabs. 'Would you let your daughter marry a Rolling Stone?' was the main thrust of Oldham's ingenious press campaign.

Offstage, from many parents' point of view, things only got worse, as The Stones seemingly challenged the Establishment by flaunting their bad-boy image, culminating in several notorious and widely reported incidents.

In the recording studio it was a different story, with The Stones going from strength to strength as the 1960s began to swing and Oldham compelled Mick and Keith to write their own material. 1964 saw the band enjoy UK chart-topping success with covers of 'It's All Over Now' and 'Little Red Rooster', as well as with an eponymous debut album that included the first Jagger/Richards composition, 'Tell Me'. They kicked off

1965 with the self-penned No. 1 'The Last Time' and followed this up with the worldwide smash that would become their anthem, '(I Can't Get No) Satisfaction', as well as the chart-topping 'Get Off Of My Cloud'.

Experimentation reared its head in 1966 with a variety of instruments on the groundbreaking *Aftermath* album (the first to contain all-original material).

Two albums later Allen Klein replaced Oldham as their manager and they released the superb 'Jumpin' Jack Flash' single and musically eclectic *Beggar's Banquet* LP (both 1968). On 9 June 1969, Jones was fired and Mick Taylor was drafted in his place, but just over three weeks later Brian Jones was found drowned in his swimming pool.

The *Let It Bleed* album and 'Honky Tonk Women' single (both 1969) maintained the run of chart success.

Exile On Main St. (1972), was recorded in the basement of a villa Richards rented in the South of France when the band were on a self-imposed exile

from Britain – it's now considered the band's masterpiece. In 1974 Taylor left and was replaced by Ron Wood, and Bill Wyman departed in 1991. Throughout the rest of the decade and right up to the present day, the band would continue to lead the way, continually redefining the standards for lavish, large-scale stadium tours and releasing new albums.

'I thought rock'n'roll was an unassailable outlet for some pure and natural expression of rebellion.' **Keith Richards**

Simon and Garfunkel

Santana

(Vocal/instrumental group, 1967–present)

A Latin-American take on what became known as jazz rock, the group led by Mexican Carlos Santana (guitar) were a palpable hit at Woodstock in 1969. This coincided with an eponymous debut album penetrating the US Top 10. An optimum commercial period – embracing US chart-toppers *Abraxas* and *Santana III* – was followed by dwindling success until 'Smooth' from 1999's guest star-studded *Supernatural* spent weeks at No. 1 in the US and elsewhere, sparking an on-going reversal of fortune.

Simon And Garfunkel

(Vocal duo, 1957–71, 1981–83, 2003–04, 2009–10)

As 'Tom and Jerry', Paul Simon (vocals, guitar) and Art Garfunkel (vocals) had a minor US Hot 100 success as teenagers in 1957 with 'Hey Schoolgirl'. Both attempted to forge solo careers, which took Simon to the UK where he became a reliable draw in the country's folk clubs. Back in the US by 1964, he recorded an album, *Wednesday Morning 3am,* with Garfunkel. Its highlight was 'The Sound Of Silence', which was issued (with superimposed backing) as a single to top the US charts. With Simon taking most of the creative initiative, later hits included 'Homeward Bound', 'Mrs Robinson' (from 1968's *The Graduate* film soundtrack) and 'The Boxer'. The new decade began with a No. 1 in both Britain and the States with 'Bridge Over Troubled Water', in which Garfunkel's breathy tenor floated effortlessly over orchestrated accompaniment. Both he and Simon have given good individual accounts of themselves in the charts since, and, if not all smiles, occasional reunions on disc and on stage have proved lucrative.

Sly And The Family Stone

(Vocal group, 1967–83, 2006)

An early 1969 single 'Everyday People' became the group's first US No. 1. It was from their fourth LP, the upbeat masterpiece *Stand!*. But just as things were coming good they started to go bad. Sly was developing a serious cocaine habit and although two cheerful singles – 'Hot Fun In The Summertime' and 'Thank You (Falletinme Be Mice Elf Agin)' – and a stop-gap *Greatest Hits* LP all charted well, it was clear that something was seriously wrong.

The much-delayed LP, *There's A Riot Goin' On*, that finally emerged in November 1971 was as dark as its predecessor had been bright. However, the album and the first single from it ('Family Affair') were the US No. 1s that Christmas.

Sly focused temporarily for 1973's *Fresh*; it and the accompanying single 'If You Want Me To Stay' made the Top 10. However, *Fresh* was Sly Stone's last great album.

Small Faces

(Vocal/instrumental group, 1965–69, 1975–78)

After entering the UK Top 20 with 1965's 'Whatcha Gonna Do About It', this pre-eminent mod group – Steve Marriott (vocals, guitar), Jimmy Winston (keyboards), Ronnie Lane (bass, vocals) and Kenney Jones (drums) – suffered a miss with self composed 'I Got Mine'; they then replaced Winston with Ian McLagan and got back on course with chart-topping 'All Or Nothing' and lesser hits before a post-1967 creative peak with 'Here Come The Nice', 'Itchycoo Park', 'Tin Soldier' and 'Lazy Sunday' (the latter from innovatively designed album *Ogden's Nut Gone Flake*), which summed up the Small Faces dialectic in its blend of R&B, psychedelia and Cockney chirpiness. 'Itchycoo Park' was the vehicle of a US advance that was thwarted by Marriott's departure to form the Humble Pie supergroup.

The others rallied by teaming up with Ron Wood (guitar) and Rod Stewart (vocals) from The Jeff Beck Group as the Faces. A brief Small Faces reunion in the late 1970s was notable for market indifference towards two comeback albums.

Phil Spector

(Producer, b. 1939)

Phil Spector devised a studio recording technique he called 'symphonies for the kids', which had considerable success in the 1960s and became known as the Wall of Sound. Characterized by mono production, it had fantastically rich choral and orchestral layering (sometimes as many as 300 musicians) behind the vocals of the titular performers he worked with.

Best remembered for his girl groups The Crystals and The Ronettes (who appear on his classic 1963 LP *A Christmas Gift For You*), he perfected his approach on The Righteous Brothers' 1965 'You've Lost That Lovin' Feelin'' and Ike and Tina Turner's 1966 'River Deep – Mountain High'. The latter's US chart failure (it reached No. 3 in Britain) shattered Spector, and he became a notoriously eccentric recluse. He has since made rare comebacks (notably with George Harrison and The Ramones). Respect for his often-imitated innovations has been overshadowed by his 2003 arrest for murder. After a 2007 mistrial, he was convicted in 2009 and given a prison sentence of 19 years to life.

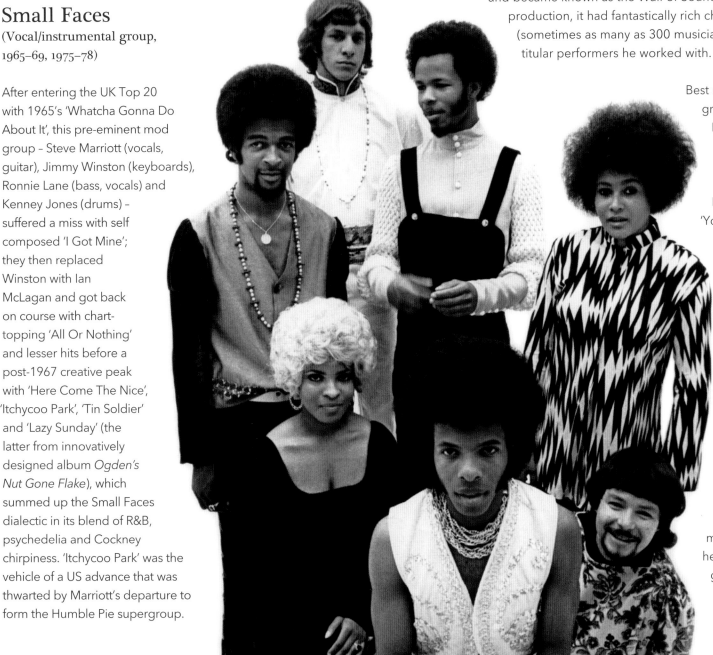

Sly and the Family Stone

Steppenwolf

Steppenwolf

(Vocal/instrumental group, 1967–72, 1974–76, 1980–present)

After they migrated from Toronto to Los Angeles, Steppenwolf scored a million-seller with the 1968 biker anthem 'Born To Be Wild'. With 'The Pusher', it was also a highlight of 1969's *Easy Rider* film soundtrack. Other hits included self-penned 'Magic Carpet Ride', 'Rock Me' and 1970's 'Hey Lawdy Mama'. Ebbing record sales led to brief disbandment in the mid-1970s, but, with German-born vocalist John Kay (Joachim Krauledat) the only original member, the group remain a potent draw on the 1960s nostalgia circuit, especially in Europe.

The Temptations

(Vocal group, 1960–present)

Formed in 1960, The Temptations were Motown's leading male group. Their first big hit was 1965's 'My Girl'. Adding psychedelic soul to the Motown pop mix, further hits included 1969's drugs-referencing 'Cloud Nine' and the civil-rights appeal of 1972's epic 'Papa Was A Rolling Stone'.

Otis Williams is the only original Temptation in the current line-up, which still tours the oldies circuit.

Traffic

(Vocal/instrumental group, 1967–69, 1970–74, 1994)

From various also-ran beat groups, Dave Mason (vocals, guitar), Chris Wood (woodwinds) and Jim Capaldi (drums) joined forces with Steve Winwood (vocals, keyboards, guitar) of The Spencer Davis Group. Though 'Paper Sun', 'Hole In My Shoe' and the *Dear Mr Fantasy* (1967) LP all charted in Britain, tensions between Winwood and Mason caused the latter's brief exit early in 1968 and a permanent one after a second album, *Traffic* (1968). Capaldi and Wood's help during subsequent sessions for a proposed solo offering by Winwood came to be issued in 1970 as a Traffic album, *John Barleycorn Must Die*. The group reached a commercial summit with 1971's million-selling *Low Spark Of High-Heeled Boys* before an over-reliance on long-winded improvisations failed to mask a creative bankruptcy, though there was a return to form with 1974's *When The Eagle Flies* finale. In 1994, Winwood and the late Capaldi reformed Traffic for an album, *Far From Home,* and correlated concerts.

The Troggs

(Vocal/instrumental group, 1964–present)

After 'Wild Thing' charged into the UK chart in 1966 its follow-up, 'With A Girl Like You', penned by mainstay Reg Presley (vocals), actually seized the top spot. These were smashes in North America, too. Intermittent successes later and the recurrence of Troggs numbers in the repertoires of countless US garage bands were a solid foundation for a lucrative post-Top 40 career that has embraced a link-up with R.E.M. for 1991's *Athens To Andover* album, and a 1994 chart-topping hit revival of 1967's 'Love Is All Around' by Wet Wet Wet.

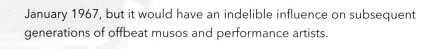

The Velvet Underground

(Vocal/instrumental group, 1964–73, 1990, 1992–94, 1996)

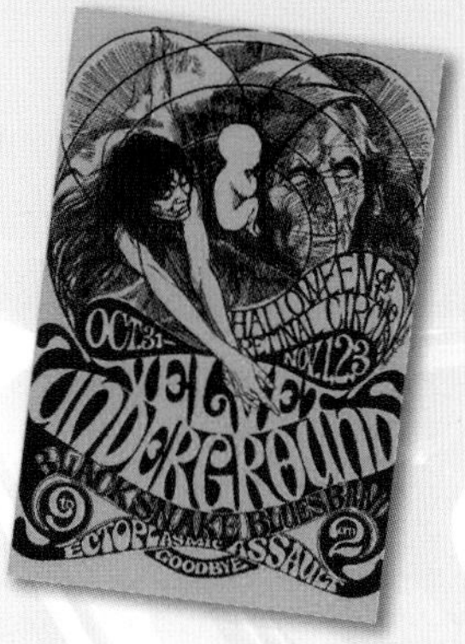

During the wildly experimental and progressive second half of the 1960s The Velvet Underground was the avant-rock outfit par excellence.

Formed by friends Lou Reed and John Cale, it was while The Velvets were performing at Café Bizarre in Greenwich Village, NY, that Pop Art guru Andy Warhol took in one of their shows and decided to manage them.

Under Warhol's guidance, and against the band members' better judgment, former model and current Warhol Factory superstar Nico was added to the line-up. Warhol then secured his protégés a contract with MGM's Verve label and, in the spring of 1966, produced their first album, *The Velvet Underground And Nico* (also known as 'The Banana Album' courtesy of his own cover art). This record's brilliantly eclectic collection of songs failed to ignite sales or light up radio dials upon its release in January 1967, but it would have an indelible influence on subsequent generations of offbeat musos and performance artists.

Nico went her own way later that year and Warhol was also out of the picture when The Velvets recorded their second album, *White Light, White Heat*, which was even more extreme and less commercially viable than their previous outing.

Not that The Velvets' instruments were the only things clashing. Reed and Cale were engaged in their own battle for artistic control, resulting in Cale's ousting from the band in 1968 and replacement by Doug Yule, who contributed bass, organ and vocals to the group's third album, *The Velvet Underground* (1969). Its quieter, more basic rock approach was also seen on 1970's *Loaded,* with relatively conventional and commercial tracks like 'Sweet Jane' and 'Rock And Roll'.

Reed, however, quit just before the album's release and he was soon followed by Morrison and Tucker, leaving Yule to front a band that was The Velvet Underground in name only by the time of its final release, the abysmal *Squeeze*, in 1973.

The Walker Brothers

(Vocal/instrumental group, 1964–68, 1975–78)

The unrelated Walkers, Scott Engel, John Maus and Gary Leeds, sought their fortunes in Britain where 'Love Her' made the Top 20 in 1965. Then came bigger smashes with 'Make It Easy On Yourself', 'My Ship Is Coming In' and 'The Sun Ain't Gonna Shine Anymore'. However, provoked by bickering between Engel and Maus, and falling sales, they went their separate ways, reforming in 1976 and scoring a UK hit with 'No Regrets'. There followed three contrasting albums.

The Who

(Vocal/instrumental group, 1964–present)

Originally comprising Pete Townshend on guitar, Roger Daltrey on vocals, John Entwistle on bass and Keith Moon on drums, The Who virtually exploded onto the mid-1960s scene in a blaze of power rock that placed them at the forefront of the mod movement.

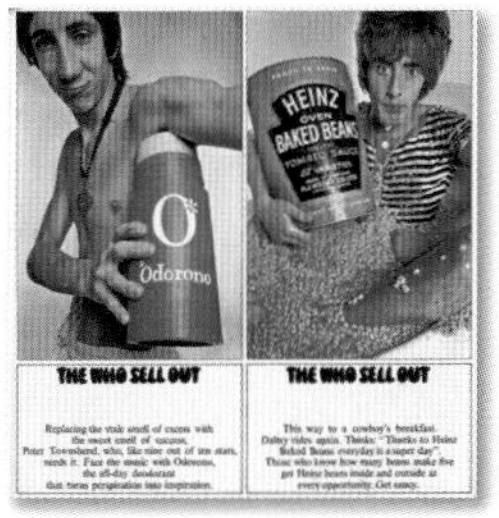

A contract with Decca Records placed the band with Kinks' producer Shel Talmy, a relationship that yielded the UK hit singles 'I Can't Explain', 'Anyway, Anyhow, Anywhere' and 'My Generation', featuring Daltrey alternately stuttering and belting out Townshend's lyrics, including the anthemic wreckless-youth line, 'I hope I die before I get old'. Onstage this message was reinforced not only by Townshend's guitar-smashing antics, but also by Keith Moon regularly demolishing his kit, and the string of UK Top 10 hits continued in 1966 with 'Substitute', although this marked the end of The Who's collaboration with Shel Talmy.

Kit Lambert now took over the production reins, and in 1967 the band at last achieved American success with *Happy Jack* (originally titled *A Quick One* in Britain). The Who had finally arrived, yet the mod movement was winding down, prompting Pete Townshend to regroup and compose what many consider to be his masterpiece, the rock opera *Tommy* (1969). It would later resurface as a play, a 1975 movie starring Daltrey, and a 1993 Broadway musical.

Thereafter, The Who would not find it easy to live up to *Tommy*'s reputation, although the band still enjoyed considerable success with further hit singles and acclaimed albums such as *Who's Next* (1971), *Quadrophenia* (1973) and *Who Are You* (1978). The latter turned out to be its last outing with Keith Moon, who died less than one month later.

The Who

And although there would be more recordings and numerous tours with others filling Moon's larger-than-life shoes, Townshend, Daltrey and Entwistle would subsequently concede that The Who really died along with its enigmatic, manically virtuosic drummer.

Stevie Wonder

(Piano, vocals, b. 1950)

Blind virtually from birth, Stevie Wonder was already singing in his local choir at the age of four. By the time he was seven he had mastered the piano, harmonica and drums. In 1961 Berry Gordy signed him up immediately and he enjoyed a succession of hits as Little Stevie Wonder.

The 1960s saw Wonder's growth in all areas from child star to soul man. He dropped the 'Little' as early as 1964, and his vocal performances developed their trademark tone.

1971's album *Where I'm Coming From* was a milestone of maturity – not just a collection of singles and album fillers but a coherent set of compositions, increasingly dominated by Wonder's keyboard arrangements and entirely produced and co-written by him. A month later, on his 21st birthday, his contract with Motown expired. Wonder negotiated a new, stronger deal that gave him increased royalties and allowed him to set up his own production and publishing companies. Most importantly he also gained complete control of his output.

Music Of My Mind, the first fruit of the new deal released early in 1972, demonstrated a further refinement of the whole-album principle, where in addition to the producing and writing credits Wonder now played all but one of the instruments.

The early 1973 album *Talking Book* was his most well-rounded and personal to date. It was followed by late 1973's outward-looking *Innervisions*. After surviving a near-fatal car crash, 1974's *Fullfillingness' First Finale* was more introspective but found time for the No. 1 political barb 'You Haven't Done Nothin'' (featuring the Jackson Five on doo-wops).

Stevie Wonder's performances on the three albums of 1973–74 earned him a total of nine Grammy Awards, enabling him in 1975 to negotiate with Motown what at the time was the richest ever recording deal: $13 million over seven years. A year later he delivered what still stands as his masterpiece, *Songs In The Key Of Life*. However, in the years that followed he struggled to emulate the artistic and commercial pinnacle of that album.

The 1980s and early 1990s saw Wonder release only a handful of albums and singles of mixed merit. But it was in 1995 that Coolio's UK and US No. 1 'Gangsta's Paradise' updated the *Songs In The Key Of Life* track 'Pastime Paradise', reminding the public of Wonder's ground-breaking work. He capitalized on the renewed attention by recording a collaboration 'How Come How Long' with contemporary producer-performer Babyface.

In 2005, at the age of 55, he released his first new album for 10 years. *A Time 2 Love* was hailed as his strongest in 25 years. It returned him to the singles charts with the stomp-funker 'So What The Fuss', and won him his 21st Grammy for his vocal performance on 'From The Bottom Of My Heart'.

The Yardbirds

(Vocal/instrumental group, 1963–68, 1992–present)

The nurtured prowess of successive lead guitarists Eric Clapton (until 1965), Jeff Beck and Jimmy Page helped make The Yardbirds one of the most innovative rock groups of the 1960s. More discreetly influential, however, were more permanent members: Keith Relf (vocals, harmonica), Chris Dreja (rhythm guitar), Paul Samwell-Smith (bass) and Jim McCarty (drums), especially after 1965's 'For Your Love' came within an ace of topping both the British and US charts, and began two years of hits that combined musical adventure and instant familiarity. In 1966, Samwell-Smith left, and Page agreed to play bass until Dreja was able to take over. Beck and Page then functioned as joint lead guitarists until the former's departure in the middle of a harrowing US tour. With an increased stake in The Yardbirds' fortunes, Page suggested the hiring of mainstream pop producer Mickie Most for the releases that preceded a final performance until McCarty and Dreja reformed the group in 1992.

Frank Zappa

(Guitar, vocals, 1940–93)

In 1964, Zappa formed The Mothers Of Invention, whose albums resembled pop-Dada aural junk-sculptures made from an eclectic heap that, laced with outright craziness, included 1950s pop, jazz, schmaltz and the pioneering tonalities of Stravinsky, Varese and Webern. However, Zappa's intense concern over social issues was never so stifled by burlesque that it

Frank Zappa

could not be taken seriously. 1968's *We're Only In It For The Money* was a chart entry but, too clever for Joe Average, the now greatly augmented Mothers were disbanded in 1970 by Zappa, who then issued *Hot Rats*, a demonstration of his guitar playing. Later projects drifted towards lavatorial humour, albeit supported by often beautiful melodies. Yet, in the decade before his death in 1993, he went some way towards establishing himself as a 'serious' composer in the same league as Varese and others of his boyhood idols – and as a professional politician, most palpably when the Czech government appointed Zappa its official Trade and Culture Emissary in 1990.

'Glamour is part of us and we want to be dandy.
We want to shock and be outrageous instantly.'

Freddie Mercury

The Seventies

The Seventies: ALL THAT GLITTERS

After the seismic shifts of the previous decade, the 1970s reflected faster moving, less permanent crazes, beginning with glam rock and ending with new wave. Of these, the arrival of punk and its nihilistic philosophy in the middle of the decade gave music a much-needed kick up the backside.

The Lure Of Profit – Everything Gets Bigger

This was the decade that saw popular music turn into one of the biggest money-making industries of recent times – record companies and acts realized their wildest dreams of fame and fortune as sales of records, concert tickets and associated merchandising went through the roof. Utopian values turned to greed as musicians abandoned their integrity to go for the big bucks.

Essential Recordings

1970 Black Sabbath: *Black Sabbath*
1971 Led Zeppelin: *Stairway To Heaven*
1973 Pink Floyd: *Dark Side Of The Moon*
1977 The Sex Pistols: *Never Mind The Bollocks*

However, this helped bring music to the masses. With a reduction in price of vinyl, all of a sudden you could buy your own records rather than share your friends'. Your listening experience became a bigger beast in the form of arena tours and as the decade was drawing to a close the compact cassette was starting to make its presence felt – along with which came the high-fidelity stereo meaning quality of sound had arrived!

Going One Step Further

The predilection for big (money-spinning) outdoor events grew even bigger, with huge festivals at Bath, the Isle of Wight, Lincoln and Weeley in the UK, whilst Watkins Glen in New York State in July 1973 saw upwards of 500,000 music fans come together.

Many musicians who rose to prominence in the 1960s became the rock Establishment of the new decade. Most of the ex-Beatles continued to sell albums and garner column inches, while Dylan returned to form. He

was joined by the likes of ex-Them singer Van Morrison, Crosby, Stills, Nash & Young, The Grateful Dead and 1960s outspoken cult figure Frank Zappa as top-grossing US-based acts of the era.

Country Rockers And Song-Singers

The return-to-roots movement that started with The Band in the late 1960s gathered momentum, especially in the UK where folk rock became hugely popular. Indeed, the move towards country & western started by the likes of The Byrds and The Flying Burrito Brothers created a new style of music: country rock. This borrowed heavily from the Nashville sound but was smoothed at the edges to create a more easy-going, radio-friendly ambience. Bands like The Eagles hit gold perfecting this style.

The early 1970s also saw the rise of the singer/songwriter, especially in the US, with Joni Mitchell, Carole King, Jackson Browne, James Taylor and Carly Simon among those matching critical acclaim with high earnings for baring their innermost souls. The UK would match them with Cat Stevens, Rod Stewart and Elton John.

Rock On

Rock in the early 1970s was hard and heavy as perfected by a new breed of British bands like Black Sabbath, Free and Deep Purple, all of whom soared to popularity with mega-selling albums in 1970–71. But undoubtedly the biggest phenomenon was Led Zeppelin who, with their mixture of bone-crushing riffs, airy acoustic interludes and stunning musicianship, became the biggest band on the planet in the1970s.

The tastes of the rock audience had swung back to alcohol and downers rather than pot and LSD, and The Rolling Stones remained superstars. Their American counterparts were the likes of The Allman Brothers, Lynyrd Skynryd and The Doobie Brothers, who all purveyed no-frills basic rock.

Mega Rock

At the other extreme was 'progressive rock', which took popular music into the realms of opera, classical and electronics. Rock became high art with supergroups like Emerson, Lake and Palmer covering classical pieces and writing long, complicated suites, while performances were taken into large arenas and stadiums with often overblown stage shows. Pink Floyd lost their arty/underground image of the 1960s to become prog megastars of the 1970s. Other kings of prog rock included Yes, King Crimson, Genesis, Jethro Tull, Queen and Mike Oldfield.

Kraftwerk

Paul Kossoff of Free

Slade

Whilst pop music had usually emanated from the shores of either Britain or America, another country became a major player in the 1970s: Germany. Here the music was of a harder, more radical hue, from the robotic sounds of Neu and Kraftwerk to the white-noise overkill of Can.

Glam-tastic

The 1970s saw the advent of glam, which had both its frivolous and serious sides. As early as 1971 the charts were alive with the sounds of Slade, T. Rex and The Sweet, all of whom played a revved-up rock dressed in sequins, sparkle and satin. The Velvet Underground had stepped out of the shadow of their mentor Andy Warhol and explored the darker side of life.

Cross-dressing and a flirtation with burgeoning gay scenes created an exciting new direction in rock. David Bowie suddenly caught on with his ambitious concept album *Ziggy Stardust And The Spiders From Mars* (1975) and bands like the New York Dolls followed in his wake.

The Black Influence And Persistence Of Pop

Black music continued to be a huge force both as an influence and as a mainstream phenomenon, with the emergence of more sophisticated and progressive forms of soul purveyed by Isaac Hayes, Gil Scott Heron, Curtis Mayfield and Stevie Wonder.

Funk was to become one of the buzzwords of the decade, combining syncopated rhythms, dominant bass lines, sharp rhythm guitars and brass. At the same time, the sound of reggae and the advent of its most famous ambassador, Bob Marley, changed the face of 1970s music.

Pop also continued to sell, thanks to the rise of acts like Elton John, Rod Stewart and Queen, all of whom crossed over from rock into the mainstream. And they may have proved culturally unimportant but the intelligent, original and wholly irresistible pop of Swedish singing quartet ABBA left an indelible mark on the pop scene. The decade was seen out with acts embracing disco – artists like Donna Summer and 1960s' rejects The Bee Gees, who completely revitalized their career writing a number of disco-based anthems.

The Dawn Of Punk

Rumours began to circulate in 1975 of a new type of rock that was a return to basics but delivered with such speed, conviction and force that it was like a blow to the head. Early influences Patti Smith and The Ramones were part of a select, incestuous scene in New York that had congregated at little clubs like CBGB in the Bowery. It was the latter band whose sound was to become the blueprint for a thousand imitators.

In London manager Malcolm McLaren and designer Vivienne Westwood, influenced by this hotbed of activity in the Big Apple, set about fashioning their own 'punks' – they created The Sex Pistols, led by a Johnny Rotten hell-bent on rejecting not just British middle-class values but all that the 1970s rock Establishment held so dear. Inevitably the big labels got in on the act and, slowly but inevitably, punk was watered down to become new wave. Biggest of all the new wavers was Blondie, whose radio-friendly pop songs climbed the charts one after another. Rock's conscience, meanwhile, was safe in the hands of the British 2-Tone bands like The Specials, whose vision was informed by inner-city decay, racism and the anti working-class policies of the incoming Thatcher government.

As the Tory party and the US Republicans came to power, the scene was set for the 1980s, an era during which, as one wag put it, it was as if punk never happened.

'Ours is the folk music of the technological age.'

Jimmy Page, Led Zeppelin

Headline Acts

ABBA

(Vocal group, 1972–82)

The most commercially successful pop band of the 1970s – formed in 1973 in Stockholm, Sweden, by Benny Andersson, Bjorn Ulvaeus and their girlfriends, Frida Lyngstad and Agnetha Faltskog (Bjorn and Agnetha eventually married and then divorced in 1979).

Winning the Eurovision Song Contest in 1974 with the song 'Waterloo', the band were propelled to the top when it became a No. 1 single in the UK and around Europe.

The next two years saw ABBA dominate the music scene globally with a string of brilliantly conceived and executed hits such as 'Mamma Mia', 'Dancing Queen' and 'Money, Money, Money'.

The group ceased after *The Visitors* (1982) but the release of *ABBA Gold* sparked a major ABBA revival that raised the band to iconic status again.

AC/DC

(Vocal/instrumental group, 1973–present)

A hard-rocking quintet whose no-frills approach garnered them a huge following, AC/DC were formed in Sydney in 1973 by expatriate Scottish brothers Angus and Malcolm Young (both guitar). Bon Scott became lead singer in 1974.

AC/DC

After two Antipodes-only albums, the band moved to America where their fifth album for Atlantic Records, *Highway To Hell* (1979), produced by Mutt Lange, established them in the big league, selling over six million copies. Its title track became a rock radio anthem.

The hard-living Scott died from alcoholic poisoning in London in February 1980 and was replaced by former Geordie singer Brian Johnson. The transition was seamless; AC/DC's first album with Johnson *Back In Black* (1980) provided their only UK No. 1. With a revolving cast of drummers and bassists, AC/DC have stuck to a winning formula, eschewing the vagaries of fashion in favour of direct, audience-pleasing rock'n'roll.

Aerosmith

(Vocal/instrumental group, 1970–present)

This best-selling American heavy rock band, frequently compared to The Rolling Stones and Led Zeppelin, centred on the relationship between principal members Steven Tyler (vocals) and Joe Perry (guitar). The pair came together in Boston, Massachusetts, with Joey Kramer (drums), Brad Whitford (guitar) and Tom Hamilton (bass). Their first album *Aerosmith* (1973) was an immediate success, paving the way for the multi-platinum *Toys In The Attic* (1974) and *Rocks* (1975).

Antagonism between Tyler and Perry led to the latter's departure in 1980, to be replaced by Jimmy Crespo. Differences were set aside four years later when Perry returned to the fold. The band's profile was raised by the ground-breaking collaboration with rappers Run DMC on the single 'Walk This Way', leading to a triumphant resurgence in Aerosmith's fortunes with *Permanent Vacation* (1987), *Pump* (1989) and *Get A Grip* (1993). Aerosmith were a key influence on 1990s American hard rock.

Aerosmith

Alice Cooper

(Vocals, b. 1948)

Although over time the name Alice Cooper came to attach itself to singer Vincent Furnier, it originally applied to the rock band that he fronted, the classic line-up of which comprised Cooper, Glen Buxton (guitar), Michael Bruce (guitar), Dennis Dunaway (bass) and Neal Smith (drums). After recording two albums for Frank Zappa's Straight label, the band relocated from California back to Detroit, developing the outrageous stage act for which Cooper became infamous.

Alice Cooper

The 1972 single and album *School's Out* made Cooper a major star in America and Britain, where his outrageous image and theatrics fitted in well with the glam rock scene. 1973's *Billion Dollar Babies* was a transatlantic No. 1 and his last work with the original band members. After several more hits, Cooper succumbed to alcoholism in the late 1970s and his star waned until the success of the 1989 album *Trash* and single 'Poison' resurrected his career.

America

(Vocal/instrumental group, 1970–present)

An Anglo-American trio formed in the UK by Gerry Beckley (guitar, vocals, keyboards), Dewey Bunnell (guitar, vocals) and Dan Peek (guitar, vocals, keyboards), sons of US military personnel and British mothers. America's acoustically backed three-part harmonies were reminiscent of Crosby, Stills and Nash. Best-known for the transatlantic 1972 hit 'Horse With No Name', the band worked with Beatles producer George Martin on four albums from 1974–77, slimming to a duo when Peek departed.

Average White Band

(Vocal/instrumental group, 1972–82, 1989–present)

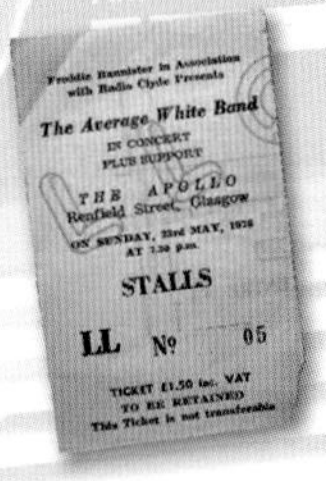

The blue-eyed soul of Scots Alan Gorrie (vocals, bass), Malcolm Duncan (saxophone), Owen McIntyre (vocals, guitar), Hamish Stuart (vocals, guitar), Roger Ball (keyboards) and Robbie McIntosh (drums) topped the US charts in 1975 with the album *AWB* and single 'Pick Up The Pieces'. After dabbling in disco with 'Let's Go Round Again', a British hit in 1980, the band went on hiatus in the mid-1980s, reforming in 1989.

Jeff Beck

(Guitar, vocals, b. 1944)

Regarded as one of Britain's finest rock guitarists, Beck left The Yardbirds in 1968 to form The Jeff Beck Group, initially featuring Rod Stewart on vocals. The band's second incarnation made two ground-breaking albums that mixed rock and pop with jazz and R&B. In 1972, the guitarist became part of the short-lived power trio Beck, Bogert and Appice before making an all-instrumental jazz-fusion album *Blow By Blow* (1975) and a collaborative work with keyboardist Jan Hammer, 1976's *Wired*. After a live album with Hammer's group in 1977, Beck did not record again until 1980's *There And Back*.

His career in the 1980s and 1990s was sporadic, littered with guest appearances, notably on Tina Turner's *Private Dancer* (1984) and Jimmy Page and Robert Plant's *Honeydrippers Vol. 1* (1984). Latterly, he has developed a new style, mixing electronics with his familiar blues rock playing.

The Bee Gees

The Bee Gees

(Vocal group, 1958–2003, 2009–12)

By adapting their songwriting and sublime harmonies to different trends over four decades, The Bee Gees have maintained a hugely successful and lucrative career. The Gibb brothers – Barry and twins Robin and Maurice – moved to Australia with their parents in 1958.

Moving back to the UK in 1967 and with manager Robert Stigwood, their first single, 'New York Mining Disaster 1941', was a Top 20 hit in the UK and the US. It was the first of 10 hits over the next two years.

After an attempt at solo careers in 1969 the trio reunited in 1971, scoring US hits that year with 'Lonely Days' and 'How Can You Mend A Broken Heart'. But it wasn't until the funk-driven *Main Course* (1975) that they really made their mark on the rising disco boom with 'Jive Talkin''. More hits followed from *Children Of The World* (1976).

The *coup de grâce* came from the soundtrack *Saturday Night Fever* (1978), which topped the US charts for 24 weeks and the UK charts for 18 weeks.

The Bee Gees failed to make the switch from disco to dance in the early 1980s and their hits tailed off. However, they continued to write hits for Diana Ross ('Chain Reaction') and Kenny Rogers/Dolly Parton ('Islands In The Stream').

Their own fortunes revived again with *ESP* (1987) and the worldwide hit 'You Win Again'. In the 1990s they released the multi-million-selling *Size Isn't Everything* (1993), *Still Waters* (1997) and the live *One Night Only* (1998).

After the sudden death of Maurice on 12 January 2003 from complications arising from a twisted intestine, Barry and Robin retired The Bee Gees' name.

Black Sabbath

(Vocal/instrumental group, 1968–present)

Pioneers of heavy metal, Sabbath hailed from Birmingham, England and comprised John 'Ozzy' Osbourne (vocals), Tony Iommi (guitar), Terence 'Geezer' Butler (bass), and Bill Ward (drums). Their second album's title track 'Paranoid' was a rare hit single as Black Sabbath's reputation was built on a series of 1970s albums, featuring doom-laden lyrics set to downtuned guitar. Osbourne was fired in 1979, finally rejoining his colleagues in 1997.

Black Sabbath

Blondie

(Vocal/instrumental group, 1974–82, 1997–present)

An internationally popular New York outfit emerging from the city's thriving new wave scene of the mid-to late 1970s, Blondie's founders were Debbie Harry (vocals) and Chris Stein (guitar), with an eventual supporting cast of Clem Burke (drums), Nigel Harrison (bass), Jimmy Destri (keyboards) and Frank Infante (guitar). More pop-oriented than their contemporaries and influenced by 1960s girl groups like The Shangri-Las, Blondie had a British No. 2 hit with 'Denis' from their second album *Plastic Letters* (1978). The follow-up, *Parallel Lines* (1978), was a chart topper on both sides of the Atlantic and contained the disco-flavoured smash 'Heart Of Glass', the first of six UK No. 1 singles.

Blondie dabbled in reggae ('The Tide Is High'), calypso ('Island Of Lost Souls') and can claim to have made the first white rap song, 'Rapture'. After the lacklustre *The Hunter* (1982), Blondie disbanded. The group reformed 15 years later and hit the UK No. 1 spot again with 'Maria'.

Debbie Harry of Blondie

Boston

(Vocal/instrumental group, 1976–present)

The all-conquering first album *Boston* released in 1976 became the biggest-selling debut of all time and yielded the hit single 'More Than A Feeling'. The follow up, *Don't Look Back* (1978), exactly duplicated its predecessor's formula, with the album selling seven million copies.

Eight years later, Boston's next album, *Third Stage* (1986), emerged boasting the US No. 1 single 'Amanda'. For 1994's *Walk On* Brad Delp was replaced as vocalist by Fran Cosmo, although he returned for *Corporate America* (2002). Delp committed suicide in 2007.

David Bowie

(Vocals, b. 1947)

One of the great chameleon figures in rock, David Bowie has also been among the most influential.

In 1969 Bowie caught the British public's imagination with the quirky 'Space Oddity' which became a Top 5 hit. Despite fuelling publicity with his androgynous image, Bowie's career continued to stutter with *The Man Who Sold The World* (1971) and *Hunky Dory* (1972) until he created the messianic rock star character Ziggy Stardust. The concept album *The Rise And Fall Of Ziggy Stardust And The Spiders From Mars* (1972) formed the basis of a theatrical live show and was a Top 5 UK album. His band – Mick Woodmansey (drums), Trevor Bolder (bass) and especially Mick Ronson (guitar, keyboards, vocals) – were dependable sidekicks.

Aladdin Sane topped the UK charts in 1973, but just weeks later Bowie dramatically killed off Ziggy live on stage in London.

After an interlude with *Pin-Ups* (1973), a covers album, Bowie returned with *Diamond Dogs* (1974), which broke America, and *Young Americans* (1975), which brought him a US No. 1 single with 'Fame' (co-written with John Lennon). By *Station To Station* (1976) Bowie's stage persona had metamorphosed into the 'Thin White Duke'.

Low (1977), recorded whilst he was in Berlin with Brian Eno, was another radically different musical direction. It was the first of a trilogy with *Heroes* (1977) and *Lodger* (1978).

Back in New York he recorded the paranoid *Scary Monsters* (1980). He also collaborated with Queen for their 'Under Pressure' hit and Bing Crosby for the 'Peace On Earth'/'Little Drummer Boy' single, as well as taking the lead role in Broadway play *The Elephant Man*, and writing film themes and soundtracks.

He returned to the mainstream with *Let's Dance* (1983) but for the rest of the decade Bowie divided his time between music, acting and soundtracks.

Continuing to make music today, he remains an icon and few rock acts of the past 30 years have been unaffected by his legacy.

The Clash

Chic

(Vocal/instrumental group, 1976–83, 1990–92, 1996, 1998–present)

Chic were a disco outfit built around the songwriting and production team of Nile Rodgers (guitar) and Bernard Edwards (bass), who were originally part of a New York rock band but changed direction when unable to secure a record deal. Chic evolved from demos recorded by the pair that formed the basis of their first album *Chic* (1977), for which drummer Tony Thompson and singer Norma Jean Wright were drafted in. Lead-off single 'Dance, Dance, Dance (Yowsah, Yowsah, Yowsah)' was a smash. Additional vocalist Luci Martin was added as Chic went on tour.

C'est Chic (1978) and *Risqué* (1979) were textbook examples of disco, spawning massive hit singles in 'Le Freak', 'I Want Your Love' and 'Good Times'. The latter became the rhythmic base for the early rap/hip-hop song 'Rapper's Delight' by the Sugarhill Gang. Chic drifted apart in the early 1980s but reformed in 1990. Edwards died in 1996.

The Clash

(Vocal/instrumental group, 1976–86)

After numerous line-up changes The Clash finally settled with Mick Jones (guitar), Paul Simonon (bass), Keith Levene (guitar), Topper Headon (drums) and Joe Strummer (vocals).

Their debut *The Clash* (1977) was one of the definitive punk albums, featuring the rallying anthem 'White Riot' and caustic rockers 'London's Burning' and 'Janie Jones'. CBS Records did not release the album in America although it sold an unprecedented 100,000 on import.

Give 'Em Enough Rope (1978), their second release, entered the UK charts at No. 2 and gave them their first Top 20 single with 'Tommy Gun'. The Clash went into creative overdrive for the eclectic but stylish double album *London Calling* (1979), which they insisted on selling for the price of a single LP. This time they cracked the US Top 30 and had a hit single with 'Train In Vain'. They over-reached their creativity on the self-produced triple album *Sandinista!* (1980).

Combat Rock (1982) refocused their energy with a big rock sound and their best songwriting on 'Rock The Casbah', 'Straight To Hell' and 'Should I Stay Or Should I Go'. In September 1983, Headon was fired for continued heroin use. Several albums later it became apparent they had lost their way and Strummer and Simonon broke up the band early in 1986.

The posthumous legacy of The Clash continued to grow. *The Story Of The Clash Volume 1* (1988) made the UK Top 10. In 1991 the reissued 'Should I Stay Or Should I Go' gave them the UK No. 1 hit they had never come close to during their career. *From Here To Eternity: Live* (1999) was another UK Top 20 album. But, in contrast to their peers, they continued to resist lucrative offers to reform right up until the sudden death of Joe Strummer from a heart attack on 22 December 2002.

George Clinton

(Vocals, b. 1941)

Born in North Carolina and raised in New Jersey, Clinton became a funk legend but his first musical venture was the five-man doo-wop group The Parliaments, formed in the late 1950s. After recording for various small labels, and following a spell in which Clinton worked for Motown, the first flowering of his later direction appeared on The Parliaments' 1967 American Top 20 single '(I Wanna) Testify'. Contractual difficulties over the group's name prompted Clinton to record with The Parliaments' backing band, newly christened Funkadelic to reflect their psychedelic side. Clinton then set up the collective of musicians that operated under the banner of Parliament/Funkadelic in the 1970s.

Onstage, as lead singer of Parliament, Clinton was a consummate showman indulging his penchant for bizarre costumes. Clinton's best-known song is Funkadelic's 'One Nation Under A Groove', a Top 10 UK hit in 1979. He launched a solo career in 1981.

Elvis Costello

(Guitar, singer/songwriter, b. 1954)

One of new wave's most celebrated songwriters, Costello (born Declan Patrick MacManus) initially portrayed himself as an angry, revenge-obsessed young man before steadily maturing into a genre-straddling elder statesman. His cheeky appropriation of the name 'Elvis' was in tune with the iconoclastic mood of 1977, when his debut album *My Aim Is True* was released. Temporary backing band Clover were superseded by

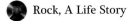

The Attractions – Bruce Thomas (bass), Steve Nieve (real name Nason, keyboards) and Pete Thomas (drums) – and their early work together, *This Year's Model* (1978) and *Armed Forces* (1979), established Costello as a major artist.

1980's *Get Happy* embraced soul music whilst an album of country covers, *Almost Blue* (1981), signalled expansive musical horizons. Costello went on to work in a variety of genres and with various collaborators; these include the Brodsky (string) Quartet, songwriter Burt Bacharach, opera singer Anne-Sofie von Otter and New Orleans musician Allen Toussaint. Costello's third wife is jazz pianist Diana Krall.

The Damned

(Vocal/instrumental group, 1976–present)

A trailblazing outfit responsible for the first British punk single, 'New Rose' in 1976, and album *Damned, Damned, Damned* (1977), the original line-up of Dave Vanian (real name Letts, vocals), Brian James (guitar), Captain Sensible (Ray Burns, bass) and Rat Scabies (Chris Miller, drums) disintegrated after the second album *Music For Pleasure* (1978). They reformed shortly afterwards, minus James, and with changing personnel since. The Damned progressed beyond punk to embrace psychedelia in the mid-1980s, their most successful period commercially.

Deep Purple

(Vocal/instrumental group, 1968–76, 1984–present)

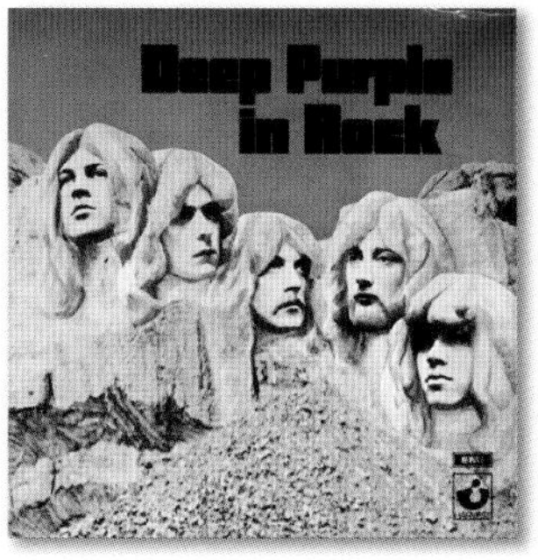

Deep Purple have sold over 100 million records in a 38-year career – continuous apart from a hiatus between 1976 and 1984 – so are one of the more commercially successful rock bands in history. Though classed as contemporaries of fellow early 1970s trailblazers Led Zeppelin and Black Sabbath, Purple were distinctly different, drawing on classical, jazz, R&B and (later) funk roots. They let live performance spread the word and cut one of the all-time classic concert albums in 1972's *Made In Japan*, which included air-guitar anthem 'Smoke On the Water'.

Their classic line-up captured on 1970's *In Rock* was Ritchie Blackmore (guitar), Jon Lord (keyboards), Ian Gillan (vocals), Ian Paice (drums) and Roger Glover (bass). The latter three were still in harness in 2006 with Don Airey (keyboards) and sole American Steve Morse (guitar), and now play extensively to South American and former Iron Curtain countries, where their popularity endures.

Dr. Feelgood

(Vocal/instrumental group, 1971–present)

A London rhythm & blues band that emerged from the pub rock scene in 1974, Dr. Feelgood's back to basics approach foreshadowed punk. Comprising Lee Brilleaux (Lee Collinson, vocals), Wilko Johnson (John Wilkinson, guitar), John B. Sparks (bass) and John 'The Big Figure' Martin (drums), their live album *Stupidity* was a 1976 chart topper. Brilleaux remained as the only original member until his death in 1994 when the band continued, in name only, with other musicians.

Nick Drake

(Guitar, singer/songwriter, 1948–74)

Although he only produced three albums before his untimely death from a drug overdose, posthumously he has become one of the most beautifully introspective and melancholic artists to come out of the 1970s. Signed to Island records at just 20, there was high hopes for the talented singer/songwriter. Whilst he was still studying at Cambridge University he released his debut, *'Five Leaves Left'* (1969), which showcased his immense skill as a self-taught guitarist and songwriter, invoking heart-warming melodies sprinkled with his 'doomed romantic' lyrics. Over the next three years he released two more albums – *Bryter Layter (1970) and Pink Moon* (1972). However, crippled with shyness that was fuelled by LSD and cannabis, he eventually disappeared from the music scene. The lack of photos or footage of the singer has only added to the mystique surrounding him and his music.

Deep Purple

The Eagles

(Vocal/instrumental group, 1971–80, 1994–present)

The band formed out of the Los Angeles country rock scene in 1971 when guitarist Glenn Frey, drummer Don Henley, guitarist Bernie Leadon and bassist Randy Meisner were recruited as Linda Ronstadt's group. They came to London to record their debut album, *The Eagles* (1972), which went gold in America, spawning three hit singles: 'Witchy Woman', 'Take It Easy' and 'Peaceful Easy Feeling'.

They returned to London for *Desperado* (1973), a conceptual album, with 'Tequila Sunrise' becoming one of their most popular songs. For *On The Border* (1974) they added guitarist Don Felder to the line-up and their slicker, sharper sound brought them their first US No. 1 with 'Best Of My Love'. *One Of These Nights* (1975) established The Eagles as one of America's biggest bands. In 1976 Leadon left the group and was replaced by guitarist Joe Walsh.

Hotel California (1976) was The Eagles' pinnacle. Painstakingly recorded, it was No. 1 in America for eight weeks, produced two No. 1 singles – 'New Kid In Town' and the title track – and won five Grammy Awards.

Meisner bailed out in late 1977. His replacement was bassist Timothy B. Schmit. *The Long Run* (1979) continued to break the band's own records, spending nine weeks at No. 1. But by the time *Live* (1980) came out the band had broken up.

The group members spent the next decade pursuing solo careers and whenever Henley was asked when The Eagles would reform he replied, 'When Hell freezes over'.

Hell Freezes Over (1994) was the result of two years inching towards a reunion. There were four new songs plus tracks from the MTV concert that launched their comeback. Since then they have toured periodically, sacked Don Felder and recorded the all-new *Long Road Out Of Eden* (2007). Meanwhile *Eagles: Their Greatest Hits 1971–75* (1975) continues to sell and has already notched up over 28 million copies.

Echo And The Bunnymen

(Vocal/instrumental group, 1978–93, 1997–present)

A post-punk quartet originating in Liverpool's thriving late 1970s new wave scene, comprising Ian McCulloch (vocals), Will Sergeant (guitar), Les Pattinson (bass) and Pete DeFreitas (drums). Career highlights include the moodily atmospheric 1980 debut *Crocodiles* and the lushly epic *Ocean Rain* (1984), but mainstream acceptance eluded them and the band split up in 1988, reforming nine years later minus DeFreitas, who perished in a motorcycle accident in 1989.

Electric Light Orchestra

(Vocal/instrumental group, 1970–83, 1985–86, 2000–01, 2012)

Devised by Roy Wood (various instruments, vocals) to provide an alternative outlet to The Move, ELO consisted of that group's remaining members, Jeff Lynne (guitar, piano, vocals) and Bev Bevan (drums). ELO aimed to combine rock with classical instrumentation. Bill Hunt (French horn) and Steve Woolam (violin) were brought in for *Electric Light Orchestra* (1971) (known as *No Answer* in the US), after which Wood left to form Wizzard and Lynne took over at the helm. Re-emerging in 1973, after further line-up changes, with a cover of Chuck Berry's 'Roll Over Beethoven', ELO embarked on a run of 15 consecutive UK Top 10 singles and regularly charted in the US with their distinctive symphonic rock.

ELO ended when Lynne left in 1986. Drummer Bev Bevan reformed the group in 1991 as ELO Part 2 when Lynne declined to participate and objected to the use of the original name.

Emerson, Lake And Palmer

(Vocal/instrumental group, 1970–79, 1991–98)

A British supergroup, who pioneered progressive rock in the early 1970s, comprising former Nice keyboardist Keith Emerson, Greg Lake, latterly of King Crimson (guitar, bass, vocals) and ex-Atomic Rooster drummer Carl Palmer. ELP's music was a fusion of classical music and rock, which Emerson had begun to explore in The Nice. Most of the band's lyrics were written by former King Crimson wordsmith Peter Sinfield. ELP made their first major appearance at the Isle of Wight Festival in 1970, releasing their self-titled debut album later that year. The immensely popular *Tarkus* followed in 1971 and the band's third album was a live rendition of Mussorgsky's *Pictures At An Exhibition* (1972).

Their best-known work, 1973's *Brain Salad Surgery,* was dominated by the epic 'Karn Evil 9'. Notorious for their extravagant live shows, ELP fell from fashion during the punk era, disbanding in 1979 but reforming in the 1990s.

Electric Light Orchestra

Fleetwood Mac

(Vocal/instrumental group, 1967–present)

After gaining cult status with blues guitarist Peter Green at the helm, his departure in 1970 saw their sound head in a more rockier direction with the addition of guitarist Lindsey Buckingham and vocalist Stevie Nicks in 1974. This new line-up helped them achieve new heights of success with their eponymous album in 1975. Internal wranglings due to affairs, drink and drugs helped pave the way for their most successful album *Rumours* (1977) – capturing their internal turmoil, this gave birth to some of their biggest hits. Over the next three decades they released a succession of albums, with *Tango In The Night* (1987) being the last with Buckingham – who left to pursue a solo career – and their first big hit since *Rumours*. However, in 2013 they announced their reunion as the *Rumours* line-up minus Christine McVie.

Fleetwood Mac

Free

(Vocal/instrumental group, 1968–71, 1972–73)

Comprising Paul Rodgers (vocals), Simon Kirke (drums), Paul Kossoff (guitar) and Andy Fraser (bass), Free made headlines in 1970. After two respected albums, *Tons Of Sobs* (1968) and *Free* (1969), had been promoted in Britain and, via a support slot to Eric Clapton's supergroup Blind Faith, the States, their primal blues rock power made them the stars of the year's Isle of Wight Festival. Hit single 'All Right Now' reached No. 2, and all looked set for lasting stardom.

But *Highway* (1970), a hurried follow-up to No. 2 hit album *Fire And Water* (1970), failed to break the UK Top 40, Kossoff's drug problems spiralled, songwriters Rodgers and Fraser clashed and a potentially world-beating band limped to a sorry conclusion in 1973. Rodgers and Kirke, the only originals, continued in Bad Company, who stripped out the commercial aspects of Free's raw blues and turned them into radio and stadium-friendly chest-beaters; Rodgers recently fronted a reformed Queen, while Kossoff died in 1976, one of British rock's most grievously wasted talents.

Generation X

(Vocal/instrumental group, 1976–81)

A London punk band consisting of Billy Idol (vocals), Tony James (bass), Bob Andrews (guitar) and Mark Laff (drums), Generation X were viewed with suspicion by the punk cognoscenti for their pop leanings and failure to toe the party line. They scored a Top 20 hit with 'King Rocker' in 1979 but otherwise their success was limited, and after three albums (one as Gen X) they split up.

Genesis

(Vocal/instrumental group, 1967–98, 2006–present)

The core of Genesis – Peter Gabriel (vocals), Tony Banks (keyboards) and Mike Rutherford (bass) – met at school in the mid-1960s. Steve Hackett (guitar) and Phil Collins (drums) joined in 1970 to complete the classic line-up, which recorded *Nursery Cryme* (1971), *Foxtrot* (1972) and *Selling England By The Pound* (1973), albums whose complex songs characterized English progressive rock.

Tensions between Gabriel and his colleagues following the ambitious concept album *The Lamb Lies Down On Broadway* (1974) saw the singer quit to be replaced at the microphone by the slightly reluctant Collins.

Peter Gabriel of Genesis

Trick Of The Tail (1976) became the band's biggest US success so far. Genesis continued to prosper as a trio when Hackett departed after 1977's *Wind And Wuthering*.

In the 1980s, a more radio-friendly approach yielded the band's most commercially successful period. Collins left in 1997 and Genesis made one more album with singer Ray Wilson. Collins, Rutherford and Banks reunited for live work in 2007.

Al Green
(Vocals, b. 1946)

An American soul and gospel singer, Reverend Al Green (he was ordained a pastor of the Full Gospel Tabernacle in Memphis in 1976) made his recording debut on *Back Up Train* (1967). His third album *Al Green Gets Next To You* (1970) was the start of a golden period when he recorded many of the songs for which he is best known – 'Tired Of Being Alone', 'Let's Stay Together' and 'Take Me To The River'.

George Harrison
(Guitar, vocals, 1943–2001)

Harrison initially became the most successful solo Beatle with the blockbuster triple album *All Things Must Pass* (1971) and the transatlantic chart topper 'My Sweet Lord'. George diverted himself into raising funds for the disaster in Bangladesh with an all-star charity gig at New York's Madison Square Garden in August 1971. The event was commemorated in the triple live set *Concert For Bangladesh* (1971). He resumed his recording career with 1972's *Living In The Material World*. *Dark Horse* (1974), *Extra Texture* (1975) and *Thirty-Three And A Third* (1976) suffered from diminishing results and he took a sabbatical after 1982's poorly received *Gone Troppo*.

Harrison bounced back with *Cloud Nine* (1987) and the smash hit 'Got My Mind Set On You'. Soon afterwards, he founded the all-star outfit Traveling Wilburys. His last solo studio album would be *Brainwashed* (2002), released a year after his death from cancer in 2001.

Hawkwind

(Vocal/instrumental group, 1969–78, 1979–present)

Purveyors of space rock since the late 1960s, Hawkwind were formed in the hippy community of London's Ladbroke Grove. The band's line-up has rarely remained stable for long but at the time of the surprise UK No. 3 'Silver Machine' in 1972, the core members were ever-present founder Dave Brock (guitar, vocals), Nik Turner (saxophone, vocals), Del Dettmar (synthesizer), Dik Mik (audio generator), Lemmy (bass, vocals), Simon King (drums) and poet/writer Robert Calvert.

1973's double live set *Space Ritual* caught Hawkwind at their peak, and a relatively stable line-up recorded *Hall Of The Mountain Grill* (1974). Fantasy author Michael Moorcock replaced Calvert, and second drummer Alan Powell and violinist Simon House were added for *Warrior On The Edge Of Time* (1975). Over the years, the band slipped into the margins but their sci-fi psychedelia and basic rhythmic throb influenced punk, heavy rock and the rave generation.

Paul Weller of The Jam

Iggy Pop

(Vocals, b. 1947)

One of the most significant figures of the 1970s, Iggy Pop (real name James Osterberg) was hailed as the godfather of punk. But when The Stooges called it a day in 1971, he was viewed as a spent force and it was only the persistence of David Bowie that led to The Stooges reconvening for *Raw Power* (1973) and a legendary gig at London's King's Cross Cinema. The band fell apart again in 1974 and Iggy entered a psychiatric institute, attempting to kick heroin. Bowie maintained contact, which led on to the pair creating Iggy's two 1977 albums *The Idiot* and *Lust For Life* in Berlin.

The burgeoning punk movement also helped re-ignite Iggy's career. 1979's *New Values* reunited him with some former Stooges colleagues and after *Zombie Birdhouse* (1982) he took a break, returning in 1986 with *Blah Blah Blah*, which again featured Bowie. He continues to record and perform.

The Jam

(Vocal/instrumental group, 1972–82)

A three-piece from Woking, Surrey, The Jam comprised Paul Weller (guitar, vocals), Bruce Foxton (bass, vocals) and Rick Buckler (drums). Emerging with punk, the band embraced the movement's energy but scorned its negative aspects. After a promising debut *In The City* (1977), the follow-up *This Is The Modern World* (1977) was rushed and unconvincing. Work on a prospective third album was scrapped, prompting a serious re-think of the band's direction.

All Mod Cons (1978) marked the start of a remarkable resurgence. 1979 saw their first Top 10 single, 'The Eton Rifles', and the quasi-concept album *Setting Sons*. The Jam swiftly became the UK's most popular group with four No. 1 singles: 'Going Underground', 'Start', 'Town Called Malice' and their final release 'Beat Surrender'. Increasingly uncomfortable with the trio's musical limitations and the demands of The Jam's huge audience, Weller disbanded the group in December 1982 to form The Style Council.

Elton John

Elton John
(Piano, vocals b. 1947)

From a shy piano player, Elton John became one of the most extrovert performers of the 1970s. He has sold over 250 million records worldwide and is now almost a national institution.

In 1967 he teamed up with aspiring lyricist Bernie Taupin and they signed to Dick James Music in 1968. Elton's first album, *Empty Sky* (1969), showed potential but it was *Elton John* (1970) that lit the fuse, particularly in America. A Top 10 single with 'Your Song' helped the album go Top 5. Between 1971 and 1976 Elton released over a dozen albums, seven of which went to No. 1 in the US along with five No. 1 singles.

Elton's flamboyant shows made him one of the top live attractions. After his first UK No. 1 single with 'Don't Go Breaking My Heart' (a duet with Kiki Dee) and the double album *Blue Moves* (1976) Elton took a break and bought Watford Football Club.

A Single Man (1978) marked a complete career change. He disbanded his partnership with Taupin, had an instrumental hit with 'Song For Guy' and generally broadened his perspectives, becoming the first pop star to tour Russia.

He continued to write major film themes (e.g. 'Can You Feel The Love Tonight' from *The Lion King* in 1994) and collaborate with other singers.

Proof of Elton's place in the nation's affections came when he sang 'Candle In The Wind' with revised lyrics at the funeral of Princess Diana in Westminster Abbey in 1997. It became the world's biggest-selling single, with sales of over 33 million. In 1998 he was knighted by the Queen for his charitable work, and in 2013 he will release his thirtieth studio album.

Joy Division
(Vocal group, 1976–80)

Their often bleak and claustrophobic music continues to inspire and influence. *Unknown Pleasures* (1979) was immediately hailed as a classic by the British music press whilst *Closer* (1980) was richer in texture but no less austere in outlook. Standalone single 'Love Will Tear Us Apart' went Top 20 but only after Curtis hanged himself in May 1980, ending the band's career.

Kiss

(Vocal/instrumental group, 1973–present)

Kiss, founded by New Yorkers Gene Simmons (bass, vocals) and Paul Stanley (guitar, vocals), combined the showmanship of glam rock and the drive of heavy metal. Recruiting Peter Criss (drums, vocals) and Paul 'Ace' Frehley (guitar, vocals) and adopting the costumes and elaborate stage make-up without which they never appeared in public, Kiss's early albums made little impact but their reputation grew via an increasingly extravagant stage show. The classic live album, 1975's *Alive,* went quadruple platinum in the States.

The ambitious *Destroyer* (1976), *Rock And Roll Over* (1976) and *Love Gun* (1977) consolidated Kiss's position as America's top rock act along with a second live set *Alive II* (1977), the fourth side of which contained new studio material. All four members released solo albums simultaneously in 1978. Criss and Frehley had departed by the time Kiss unmasked in 1983 although they, and the make-up, would return.

Kraftwerk

(Vocal/instrumental group, 1970–present)

This German electronic group's pioneering use of synthesizers made them one of the all-time most influential bands. Co-founders Florian Schneider and Ralf Hütter set up Kling Klang Studio in Düsseldorf in 1970, where the pair made three albums. They were augmented by electronic percussionists Wolfgang Flür and Karl Bartos on a tour to promote the band's fourth album *Autobahn* (1974), completing Kraftwerk's classic line-up. *Autobahn* brought the group to an international audience when the title track became a Top 30 hit in Britain and America in 1975.

The three albums that followed, *Radio-Activity* (1975), *Trans-Europe Express* (1977) and *The Man Machine* (1978) were to alter the course of popular music, highlighting the possibilities of the synthesizer as a lead instrument. Live performances played up the mechanical angle, using life-size robot replicas of the band members. Kraftwerk continue to release albums, albeit with increasingly long gaps.

Led Zeppelin

(Vocal/instrumental group, 1968–80, 1985, 1988, 1995, 2007)

The biggest heavy metal band of the 1970s, Led Zeppelin left an indelible mark that is still felt a quarter of a century later. The band was put together in London in 1968 by guitarist Jimmy Page, who recruited singer Robert Plant, bassist John Paul Jones and drummer John Bonham.

Their first album was recorded at London's Olympic Studios in 30 hours for less than £2,000 and Peter Grant, their infamous manager, took the tapes to America, where he negotiated a contract with Atlantic Records that gave the band a £200,000 advance and complete artistic control, unprecedented for an unknown group. *Led Zeppelin* (1969) contained tracks like the frenetic 'Communication Breakdown' and the slow-building, explosive 'Dazed And Confused' that featured Page playing guitar with a violin bow.

On the back of relentless touring, *Led Zeppelin* gradually climbed the US and UK album charts, eventually reaching the Top 10 without help from singles or TV appearances (the band deliberately shunned both). When *Led Zeppelin II* (1969) was released it quickly rose to No. 1 in the US and UK. *Led Zeppelin II* was recorded at various studios in breaks between tours but was mixed in a single weekend. The opening 'Whole Lotta Love' was Led Zeppelin's manifesto condensed into five and a half minutes.

Led Zeppelin III (1970) was released with advance orders that sent it to the top of the US and UK charts. *Led Zeppelin IV* (1971) – the album cover had no title, not even the band's name – is widely regarded as their finest album, featuring the epic 'Stairway To Heaven'. They played sell-out tours all over the world and in America they broke box-office records that had been set by The Beatles. *Houses Of The Holy* (1973) was the first album to get a title and left critics lukewarm, but the crowds who flocked to their concerts had no qualms, making it a No. 1 album around the world.

By now Led Zeppelin were touring America in a private jet named 'The Starship' and were the biggest grossing act in the world, with tales of their rock'n'roll excesses already entering folklore. At the beginning of 1974 they formed their own record label, Swansong, and spent much of the year working on their next album.

They returned with the double album *Physical Graffiti* (1975), which received universal acclaim.

They continued touring and released four albums between 1976–79. However, in the summer of 1980 they toured Europe and were rehearsing for an American tour when John Bonham was found dead on 25 September, having choked on his own vomit. In December the remaining band members announced that they 'could not continue as we were'. An album of unreleased recordings, *Coda*, was issued in 1982.

In 1985 the three surviving members performed as Led Zeppelin at Live Aid with drummers Phil Collins and Tony Thompson. They played together again in 1993 at Atlantic Records' 40th anniversary concert and in London in 2007 to commemorate Ahmet Ertegun's passing, both times with Bonham's son Jason on drums.

Classic Recordings

1969 Led Zeppelin II, Whole Lotta Love
1971 Led Zeppelin IV, Black Dog, Stairway To Heaven
1973 No Quarter
1975 Physical Graffiti, Kashmir

'It wasn't supposed to be a pretty thing.' **Robert Plant**

John Lennon

(Guitar, vocals, 1940–80)

Lennon's post-Beatles solo career began with *John Lennon/Plastic Ono Band* (1970), a harrowingly honest record inspired by the Primal therapy that Lennon was undergoing. *Imagine* (1971) featured his best-loved song (not released as a UK single until 1975) and was a more sugar-coated affair. The double album *Sometime In New York City* (1972) featured politically charged lyrics and received a hostile reception. The workmanlike *Mind Games* (1973) was recorded in the shadow of Lennon's separation from Yoko Ono. His infamous 'lost weekend' in LA produced 1974's *Walls And Bridges*, a partial return to form.

He was reunited with Yoko Ono in 1974 and, after the birth of son Sean in 1975, Lennon temporarily retired from music, becoming a house-husband. Shortly before his murder in 1980, he re-emerged with *Double Fantasy*, an album shared equally between Lennon and Ono. A second collaboration, *Milk And Honey*, was released posthumously in 1984.

Lynyrd Skynyrd

(Vocal/instrumental group, 1964–77, 1979, 1987–present)

This southern rock band came together in Jacksonville, Florida, around the core of Ronnie Van Zant (vocals), Allen Collins (guitar) and Gary Rossington (guitar), plus Billy Powell (keyboards), Larry Junstrom (bass) and Bob Burns (drums). An air crash shortly before the release of their sixth album *Street Survivors* in 1977 claimed the lives of Van Zant and additional guitarist Steve Gaines, although the band continued. Skynyrd remain best known for the anthemic 'Freebird'.

Bob Marley

(Guitar, vocals, 1945–81)

The man responsible for popularizing reggae worldwide, Bob Marley's career began in 1963 in the original Wailers, a six-piece vocal group, later slimmed to a trio, operating out of Kingston, Jamaica and enjoying great success locally. In 1969, Marley worked with producer Lee 'Scratch' Perry, who introduced him to the Barrett brothers – Aston (Family Man) on bass and Carlton (drums) – who would become a vital component of the new Wailers, formed in 1974.

Bob Marley

The previous year, Marley signed to Island Records, who provided promotional clout for *Catch A Fire* (1973). Eric Clapton's 1974 version of 'I Shot The Sheriff' raised Marley's profile and 'No Woman No Cry', from *Live At The Lyceum* (1975), proved his chart breakthrough. *Exodus* (1977) and *Kaya* (1978) were massive sellers internationally. *Uprising* (1980) was to be his last studio album. Since his death from cancer in 1981, Marley's reputation and influence has risen steadily.

John Martyn

(Guitar, vocals, 1948–2009)

A Scottish singer/songwriter (real name Iain McGeachy) who mixed folk, blues and jazz and developed his trademark guitar sound by use of the Echoplex, a tape delay machine, Martyn made his debut with 1968's *London Conversation* and after two albums with then wife Beverly, he released the seminal *Solid Air* (1973), a prototype ambient album. On 1980's *Grace And Danger* Martyn made the transition from solo artist to band leader; he received the OBE shortly before his death.

Paul McCartney And Wings

(Vocal/instrumental group, 1971–81)

McCartney put together Wings in the summer of 1971, featuring wife Linda (keyboards), Denny Laine (guitar) and Denny Seiwell (drums) for the debut album *Wildlife* (1971). The line-up was bolstered by the inclusion of guitarist Henry McCullough.

In 1973, Seiwell and McCullough abruptly quit, refusing to travel to Nigeria to record *Band On The Run* (1973), a commercial and artistic triumph forged in adversity. Guitarist Jimmy McCulloch and sticksman Jeff Britton joined in 1974, the latter soon replaced by Joe English. A successful world tour in 1975–76 followed but the band splintered again in 1977 when English and McCulloch departed. Undaunted, McCartney recorded 'Mull Of Kintyre', which became Britain's best-selling single. Laurence Juber (guitar) and Steve Holly (drums) were added for *Back To The Egg* (1979) but the ex-Beatle's arrest for possession of cannabis in Japan in 1980 caused a cancelled tour and the end of Wings.

Van Morrison

(Vocals, b. 1945)

After leaving Irish beat group Them, Van Morrison relocated to the States in 1967 to launch a solo career. His debut single 'Brown Eyed Girl' was a hit in America but not Britain. His second album *Astral Weeks* (1968) was a massively influential work, which added Celtic and jazz influences to his R&B and soul roots. Particularly prolific in the mid-1970s, Morrison has made over 30 albums in his career.

Van Morrison

Mott The Hoople

(Vocal/instrumental group, 1969–74, 2009)

A riotous rock band comprising Ian Hunter (vocals, keyboards), Mick Ralphs (guitar), Pete 'Overend' Watts (bass), Verden Allen (organ) and Dale 'Buffin' Griffin (drums), Mott were about to split when offered 'All The Young Dudes' by David Bowie in 1972. This began a string of five hits and two successful albums *Mott* (1973) and *The Hoople* (1974). The band split in 1974 but their enduring influence on British rock was proven by an unlikely 2009 reunion for a run of sellout London shows.

New York Dolls

(Vocal/instrumental group, 1971–77, 2004–present)

A trailblazing quintet whose energetic, shambolic style has been an enduring influence, the New York Dolls were formed in 1971 by David Johansen (vocals) and Johnny Thunders (guitar, died 1991), adding Sylvain Sylvain (guitar), Arthur Kane (bass, died 2004) and Billy Murcia (drums, died 1972 and replaced by Jerry Nolan, died 1992). The 1973 debut *New York Dolls* was promoted by a legendary appearance on British television's *The Old Grey Whistle Test*.

The album was not a big seller and record company Mercury dropped the Dolls after a similar failure of the 1974 follow-up *Too Much Too Soon*. Future Sex Pistols manager Malcolm McLaren took charge of the band's final days as they flirted with communist iconography. Folding in 1977, surviving Dolls Sylvain and Johansen released new albums in 2006 and 2009, playing festivals to acclaim.

Gary Numan
(Various instruments, vocals, b. 1958)

Originally recording as Tubeway Army – the name used on his first No. 1 single 'Are "Friends" Electric?' – Numan's electronic music was influenced by Berlin-era Bowie and set in a dystopian future of his own imagining. The hypnotic synthesizers and emotionless vocals earned him a second 1979 chart topper 'Cars', which was also a smash in America. Mainstream success proved difficult to sustain but Numan still commands a devoted cult following with a new, more industrial sound.

Mike Oldfield
(Multi-instrumentalist, b. 1953)

A prodigiously talented musician, Oldfield played all the instruments on 1973's *Tubular Bells*. This symphonic work was a transatlantic best-seller, helped by the use of its main theme in the movie *The Exorcist* (1973). *Hergest Ridge* (1974) was a British No. 1 whilst *Ommadawn* (1975) and *Incantations* (1978) displayed African and folk influences. *Platinum* (1979) marked a change of direction to individual songs. Oldfield has since reworked *Tubular Bells* several times.

Alan Parsons Project
(Vocal/instrumental group, 1977–90)

Studio engineer Parsons (b. 1948) had been involved with the engineering of The Beatles' *Abbey Road* (1969) and Pink Floyd's *The Dark Side Of The Moon* (1973) before he became a producer and, briefly, artist in conjunction with songwriter Eric Woolfson. A string of immaculately played and produced concept albums featuring guest singers and musicians, notably 1977's *I Robot* and 1982's *Eye In The Sky*, charted big in the States but remained a studio-bound operation (though Parsons toured in 1994 with a Live Project). Woolfson died in 2009.

Gary Numan

Pink Floyd

(Vocal group, 1965–95, 2005)

One of the biggest progressive rock bands of the decade, they have remained massively popular and their influence continues to be felt in rock and ambient music.

Classic Recordings

1967 *Arnold Layne*
1971 *One Of These Days*
1973 *Dark Side Of The Moon, Money*
1975 *Wish You Were Here, Wish You Were Here*
1979 *The Wall, Another Brick In The Wall Part 2, Comfortably Numb*

The band were formed in London in 1965 by singer/guitarist Syd Barrett, bassist Roger Waters, keyboard player Richard Wright and drummer Nick Mason.

Signing to EMI in 1967, the band released two quirky singles written by Barrett that made the Top 20 and Top 10 respectively. Barrett also wrote the songs on their debut album, *Piper At The Gates Of Dawn* (1967), which made No. 6 in the UK charts. By the end of 1967, however, Barrett's increasingly unstable behaviour was becoming a liability and at the beginning of 1968 the band drafted in another Cambridge friend, David Gilmour, as an additional guitarist. The idea was to ease the pressure on Barrett but this proved impractical and he left in March of that year.

During 1968 and 1970 their success was growing but it wasn't until *Atom Heart Mother* (1970) that they got their first UK No. 1 album.

Their eighth studio album, the ground-breaking concept album *The Dark Side Of The Moon* (1973), catapulted them into another league, giving them their first US No.1.

Wish You Were Here (1975) explored similar themes of madness and alienation. The 26-minute 'Shine On You Crazy Diamond' that book-ended the album was a tribute to Barrett. By now Waters was exercising increasing dominance over the group and their live show had developed into a spectacular production with quadraphonic sound, lights, film, animation and inflatable pigs hovering above the audience.

Their most ambitious release was the concept album *The Wall* (1979). The dark, dramatic soundscape featured the powerful, emotional 'Comfortably Numb' and 'Another Brick In The Wall Part 2'.

But walls were now appearing between the members of Pink Floyd. Wright was fired during the making of the album although he was re-hired for the concerts. And Gilmour and Mason had little input into the next Pink Floyd album, *The Final Cut* (1983), a caustic, heartfelt diatribe by Waters on the futility of war and tyrannical politicians. Although the album went to No. 1 in the UK (*The Wall* had only reached No. 3) it peaked at No. 6 in the US and sold markedly less than previous albums. With no shows forthcoming the band had effectively ceased. Pink Floyd returned in 1994 with *The Division Bell*, another No. 1 album in the US

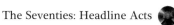

and UK. The subsequent tour was lavish, even by Pink Floyd standards, and included a complete performance of *The Dark Side Of The Moon*. It was seen by over five million people and was again documented on the live *Pulse* (1995) – also No. 1 in the US and UK.

So it was a considerable surprise in June 2005 when Bob Geldof announced that Pink Floyd – with Waters, Gilmour, Wright and Mason – would be appearing at the Live 8 Festival in London on 2 July, televised worldwide.

'For us the most important thing is to be visual.... We get very upset if people get bored when we're only halfway through smashing the second set.' **Roger Waters**

Queen

(Vocal/instrumental group, 1970–present)

Formed in London by singer Freddie Mercury, guitarist Brian May and drummer Roger Taylor, with bassist John Deacon completing the line-up in 1971, Queen started touring after the release of *Queen* (1973) and their live performances quickly won them a loyal following.

Freddie Mercury of Queen

Queen II (1974) gave the band their first UK hit with 'Seven Seas Of Rhye' but it was the tight harmonies and dynamic playing of 'Killer Queen' from their third album, *Sheer Heart Attack* (1974), that really caught the band's character and marked them out from the fading glam rock wave.

They upped their game in 1975 with the epic 'Bohemian Rhapsody'. The single, boosted by a ground-breaking video, stormed the British charts. The equally extravagant album *A Night At The Opera* (1975) also topped the UK charts and was a big international success. *News Of The World* (1977) featured two of rock's greatest anthems: 'We Will Rock You' and 'We Are The Champions'.

The Game (1980) was a deliberate pop album. It was a UK No. 1 and their biggest US success, topping the charts for five weeks with two No. 1 singles. *Greatest Hits* (1981), featuring, 'Flash', the theme song to the *Flash Gordon* movie, was a massive worldwide success, not least in the UK where it stayed in the charts for nearly eight years.

Over the next four years they kept on churning out the hits. *Innuendo* (1991), which included 'Headlong' and the grandiose 'The Show Must Go On', was to be the last release before Mercury's death of AIDS that same year. *Made In Heaven* (1995), an album of songs recorded with Mercury shortly before he died, debuted at No. 1 and became Queen's best-selling studio album. Periodically, the remaining group members revive the band for a project. In 2005 and 2006 they toured with former Bad Company vocalist Paul Rodgers and later Adam Lambert. But everyone knows Freddie Mercury can never be replaced.

The Ramones

(Vocal/instrumental group, 1974–96)

The definitive American punk rock group, The Ramones were formed in New York by high school friends Joey Ramone, Johnny Ramone, Dee Dee Ramone and Tommy Ramone.

The band signed to Sire Records in 1975. *The Ramones* (1976), a low-budget album, created a stir in the emerging punk scene. Few radio stations were bold enough to give their singles airplay, but DJ John Peel and a host of punk musicians-to-be were more impressed when they toured Britain soon after the album's release. *Leave Home* (1976) was more of the same with songs like 'You're Gonna Kill That Girl', 'Pinhead' and 'Carbona Not Glue'. They toured the US and UK frequently and cracked the UK Top 30 with 'Sheena Is A Punk Rocker' from their third album, *Rocket To Russia* (1977), which made the US Top 50 and confirmed a more bubblegum approach to their songs.

Tommy left in 1978 but stayed on to produce *Road To Ruin* (1978) featuring new drummer Marky Ramone. But it wasn't until they teamed up with Phil Spector on *End Of The Century* (1980) that they saw commercial success.

The Ramones

The band reached a hiatus when Marky left to be replaced by Ritchie Ramone and Joey underwent emergency brain surgery. But they returned with the well-received *Too Tough To Die* (1985), followed by *Animal Boy* (1986) and *Halfway To Sanity* (1986).

Then there were more line-up changes as Marky returned to replace Ritchie and Dee Dee left. The new bassist was C.J. Ramone. For the first part of the 1990s the band carried on releasing albums but failed to make a massive impact and the aptly named *Adios Amigos!* (1995) was to be their last album.

The band's irreverent attitude and three-minute songs will forever see them acclaimed as Godfathers of Punk.

Roxy Music

(Vocal/instrumental group, 1971–76, 1979–83, 2001–present)

This enduringly influential British art rock group's combination of futuristic music and 1950s rock'n'roll emerged in 1972 with their eponymous first album and standalone single 'Virginia Plain'. Fronted by singer Bryan Ferry, the line-up included synthesizer player/tape operator Brian Eno, Phil Manzanera (guitar), Andy McKay (saxophone), Paul Thompson (drums) and various bassists. When Eno left after *For Your Pleasure* (1973), Roxy's music lost some of its experimental edge but continued to plough a distinctive furrow through *Stranded* (1974) and *Country Life* (1975). Eno was replaced by classically trained keyboardist Eddie Jobson.

After *Siren* (1976), which contained their only US hit 'Love Is The Drug', Roxy Music took a break, reconvening two years later for *Manifesto*. This along with *Flesh + Blood* (1980) and *Avalon* (1983) saw the band's music take on a glossy, commercial sheen. Roxy Music disbanded in 1983 and reformed in 1998.

The Runaways

(Vocal/instrumental group, 1975–79)

A proto-punk all-girl outfit put together by LA producer/svengali Kim Fowley, The Runaways were influenced by heavy metal and the glam rock of The Sweet and Suzi Quatro. Initially comprising Cherie Curie (vocals), Joan Jett (guitar), Lita Ford (guitar), Jackie Fox (bass) and Sandy West (drums), the band made five albums and went through several line-up changes before splitting up in 1979. Jett and Ford went on to solo success.

The Runaways

The Sex Pistols

(Vocal/instrumental group, 1975–78, 1996, 2002, 2003, 2007, 2008)

The Sex Pistols came together in London under the aegis of Malcolm McLaren, who was running a boutique with Vivienne Westwood. Having unsuccessfully tried to resuscitate the ailing career of US proto-punks the New York Dolls, he turned his attention to setting up a band featuring bassist Glen Matlock, guitarist Steve Jones and drummer Paul Cook.

McLaren introduced them to singer John Lydon and called them The Sex Pistols, while the band called Lydon Johnny Rotten.

In October 1976, they signed to EMI and released a single 'Anarchy In The UK' that barely scraped into the Top 40. The group's notoriety was assured when they appeared on an early evening TV show presented by Bill Grundy, who goaded them into swearing. In the media furore that followed, EMI revoked their contract.

Matlock, who had written most of the songs, was fired in March 1977 and was replaced by Sid Vicious.

In May 1977 The Sex Pistols signed to Virgin and released 'God Save The Queen', coinciding with the Silver Jubilee celebrations. It was banned by the BBC and some retailers but still sold a reported 150,000 in the first week. It reached No. 2 in the chart.

Airplay restrictions were lifted for 'Pretty Vacant', which got to No. 6, and when *Never Mind The Bollocks* (1977) was released it went straight to No. 1.

At the beginning of 1978 Rotten quit and then in October 1978 Vicious was arrested and charged with murder after girlfriend Nancy Spungen was found dead in their hotel room. Released on bail, he died of a heroin overdose on 2 February 1979.

Rotten, Cook and Jones reunited for the 'Filthy Lucre' world tour in 1996 and released *Filthy Lucre Live*. They played more shows sporadically thereafter, but spurned their Rock and Roll Hall of Fame induction in 2006.

Siouxsie And The Banshees

(Vocal/instrumental group, 1976–96, 2002)

A legendary punk band, The Banshees did not release their first single, 'Hong Kong Garden', until 1978. Vocalist Siouxsie was accompanied by Steve Severin (bass), John McKay (guitar) and Kenny Morris (drums). McKay and Morris left abruptly in 1979 to be replaced by Budgie (ex-Slits) and John McGeoch, formerly of Magazine, whose more sophisticated, nimble-fingered guitar steered the band away from the punk assault of old and into their most popular phase.

Patti Smith
(Vocals, b. 1946)

Unorthodox, uncompromising, Patti Smith was a seminal figure in the New York punk movement and has remained a touchstone for later generations of rock artists. Starting her career writing poetry for various publications, she was eventually signed to Arista Records and released *Horses* (1975) but it wasn't until 1978 that she gained prominence with *Easter*, featuring the Bruce Springsteen-penned track 'Because The Night'. In 1980 she slowed things down and moved to Detroit to focus on her family, only to return in 1988 with *Dream Of Life*.

In 1994 her husband and brother died and her response was to return to New York and start performing again, including a tour with Bob Dylan. She confronted her life as a mother, a widow and an artist on *Gone Again* (1996) and *Peace And Noise* (1997). Smith continues to record albums – *Gung Ho* (2000), *Trampin'* (2004) – and perform. In 2007, she was inducted into the Rock and Roll Hall of Fame.

Bruce Springsteen
(Guitar, vocals, b. 1949)

Hailed as the new Dylan after two albums, Springsteen fully realized his potential with the widescreen *Born To Run* (1975). Managerial problems delayed *Darkness On The Edge Of Town* (1978), a more sombre but no less compelling work. The double album *The River* appeared in 1980 followed by the stark, pessimistic *Nebraska* in 1982.

1984's *Born In The USA* catapulted Springsteen into the mainstream, selling 14 million copies worldwide, whilst an estimated two million people saw the accompanying world tour. Backed by the E Street Band, Springsteen was without equal as a live performer, with gigs often lasting over four hours, as documented on the 1986 five-record epic *Live 1977–85*. He opted for a more intimate approach for *Tunnel Of Love* (1987), which detailed the breakdown of his first marriage and was Springsteen's last work with the E Street Band until a 1999 reunion tour.

Bruce Springsteen

Status Quo
(Vocal/instrumental group, 1967–present)

The great survivors of British rock, Quo are synonymous with three-chord boogie but first came to public attention in 1967 with the psychedelically flavoured single 'Pictures Of Matchstick Men' (their only US Top 20 hit). A change of direction to their more familiar style was heralded by the single 'Down The Dustpipe' and explored more fully on the 1970 album *Ma Kelly's Greasy Spoon*. The line-up coalesced around the ever-present duo of Francis Rossi (guitar, vocals) and Rick Parfitt (guitar) with Alan Lancaster (bass) and Richard Coughlan (drums).

Bedecked in denim and plimsolls, Quo were a potent live force, consolidating their popularity with a string of consistent albums: *Piledriver*, *Hello* (both 1973), *Quo* (1974), *On The Level* (1975) and *Blue For You* (1976). Their many hits include 'Caroline', their only UK singles chart topper 'Down Down' and the song that would open Live Aid, John Fogerty's 'Rockin' All Over The World'.

Rod Stewart
(Vocals, b. 1945)

One of the UK's finest rock vocalists, Rod Stewart trained as an apprentice footballer before becoming part of the rock star elite. Starting his career off in The Jeff Beck Group with bassist Ron Wood, the two then went on to form The Faces whilst at the same time Stewart maintained his solo career. However, everything changed with the self-produced and largely self-written *Every Picture Tells A Story* (1971) and single 'Maggie May'.

Marc Bolan of T. Rex

Through the 1980s and 1990s Stewart continued to produce commercially successful hits. In 2002, after a successful operation for thyroid cancer, Stewart embarked on a series of albums called *The Great American Songbook,* featuring guest appearances by Cher, Diana Ross, Stevie Wonder and Elton John. The series revitalized Stewart's career and *Stardust … The Great American Songbook Volume III* (2004) gave him his first US No. 1 album for 25 years.

The Stranglers
(Vocal/instrumental group, 1974–present)

Formed in 1974 in Guildford, Surrey, The Stranglers were relatively experienced musicians when they broke through at the same time as punk in 1977. Comprising Hugh Cornwell (guitar, vocals), Jean-Jacques Burnel (bass, vocals), Dave Greenfield (keyboards) and Jet Black (drums), the band's early sound was notable for The Doors-like keyboards and grumbling bass. The Stranglers' two 1977 albums *Rattus Norvegicus* and *No More Heroes* made them new wave's best-selling band. *Black And White* (1978) and *The Raven* (1979) kept their profile high.

A more experimental direction was forged with 1981's *Gospel According To The Meninblack* whilst *La Folie* (1982) yielded the band's biggest hit, 'Golden Brown'. After 10 albums, Cornwell quit for a solo career in 1990. The Stranglers remain popular on the live circuit with Paul Roberts (vocalist, left 2006) and John Ellis (guitar), who was replaced by Baz Warne (now also lead vocalist) in 2000.

T. Rex
(Vocal/instrumental group, 1967–77)

The first glam rock band evolved from acoustic duo Tyrannosaurus Rex, formed by Marc Bolan (guitar, vocals) and multi-instrumentalist Steve Peregrine-Took. Mickey Finn (bongos) replaced Took in 1969 as Bolan began to deploy electric instruments. Shortening the name to T. Rex heralded a chart breakthrough in October 1970 with the single 'Ride A White Swan'.

Steve Currie (bass) and Bill Legend (drums) were added and T. Rex achieved a further 10 Top 10 singles, including four No. 1s, as Bolan became a teen idol. The formula of speeded-up Chuck Berry riffs and Bolan's unfathomable yet hip lyrics was starting to wear thin by 1973 when T. Rex were losing ground not only to glam rivals Slade, but also to pin-up boy David Cassidy. Bolan's popularity slipped away until a new generation hailed him as one of punk's forefathers. Bolan died in a car accident in September 1977.

James Taylor

(Guitar, singer/songwriter, b. 1948)

Discovered by The Beatles' Apple label, for whom he recorded his first album in 1968, Taylor moved back to America to seek a cure for heroin addiction. He signed to Warner Bros and unleashed the three-million-selling *Sweet Baby James* in 1970, featuring the No.3 single 'Fire and Rain'. Although his early work typified the sensitive early 1970s singer/songwriter, 1977's *JT* displayed a more upbeat approach. His 1976 *Greatest Hits* collection was certified diamond for 10 million sales.

Television

(Vocal/instrumental group, 1973–78, 1992–93, 2001–present)

An art punk group formed in New York in 1973, Television originally included Richard Hell (bass), who later formed The Heartbreakers and The Voidoids, along with guitarists Tom Verlaine and Richard Lloyd, and Billy Ficca (drums). Hell soon left due to friction with Verlaine. Fred Smith, briefly a member of Blondie, took over on bass. Television became part of the nascent punk scene in New York, which centred on the legendary venues Max's Kansas City and CBGB. The interlocking guitars of Verlaine and Lloyd provided the band's trademark and set them apart from their peers.

Television

Television's first release was a pioneering independent single, 'Little Johnny Jewel'. The debut album *Marquee Moon* (1977) was immediately hailed by critics as a classic but the band split after the disappointing follow-up, *Adventure* (1978). Television reformed in 1992 for a third, eponymous album and have performed together occasionally since.

Thin Lizzy

(Vocal/instrumental group, 1969–84, 1996–2001, 2004–present)

This Irish hard rock band were led by the charismatic Phil Lynott (bass, vocals), with Brian Downey (drums) and, for the classic line-up, the twin lead guitars of Scott Gorham and Brian Robertson. The 1976 smash 'The Boys Are Back In Town' marked the start of the band's golden period, culminating in the classic *Live And Dangerous* (1978). Thin Lizzy split in the 1980s and Lynott died in 1986.

Tina Turner

(Vocals, b. 1939)

An American soul/rock singer, Tina Turner was famous initially as part of a husband-and-wife duo with Ike Turner. The pair enjoyed several hits in the 1960s and established a formidable reputation as a live act, largely due to Tina's stage presence. The couple's last major success was 1973's 'Nutbush City Limits', a UK Top 5 hit written by Tina. Weary of Ike's mental and physical abuse, she left him mid-tour in 1976, embarking on a solo career soon afterwards.

It was not until *Private Dancer* (1984) that Tina found the formula that would make her one of the biggest names in 1980s music. Made with the assistance of famous friends like Mark Knopfler and Jeff Beck, the album sold over 20 million copies. The successful follow-ups *Break Every Rule* (1986) and *Foreign Affair* (1989) showed that her remarkable comeback was no flash in the pan.

Yes

(Vocal/instrumental group, 1968–81, 1982–2004, 2008–present)

The quintessential progressive rock outfit, Yes were formed in late-1960s London by bassist Chris Squire, singer Jon Anderson and drummer Bill Bruford. Early albums *Yes* (1969) and *Time And A Word* (1970) only hinted at their potential. *The Yes Album* (1970) featured new guitarist Steve Howe and established them as a major force with virtuoso musicianship, epic songs and Anderson's unique voice and lyrics. The classic line-up was completed when keyboard maestro Rick Wakeman joined for *Fragile* (1971). 1972's *Close To The Edge* saw Yes at the peak of their powers.

Alan White replaced Bruford on *Tales From Topographic Oceans* (1973), a double set containing four side-long compositions. Disillusioned by the band's direction, Wakeman left to be replaced by Patrick Moraz on *Relayer* (1974). He returned for 1977's *Going For The One*. Personnel changes continued to bedevil Yes through the 1980s and 1990s, with Squire the only ever-present member.

Neil Young

Neil Young

(Guitar, vocals, b. 1945)

This highly respected Canadian musician first came to prominence in 1967 as a member of Buffalo Springfield. Young's solo career began in 1969 with *Neil Young*. For his next album, *Everybody Knows This Is Nowhere* (1969), he recruited Danny Whitten (guitar), Billy Talbot (bass) and Ralph Molina (drums), collectively known as Crazy Horse. Shortly afterwards, Young joined Crosby, Stills and Nash for an album and tour.

1972's country-tinged 'solo' album *Harvest* was a huge seller, but darkness engulfed Young's work following the sacking and subsequent death by overdose of Whitten, as reflected in *Time Fades Away* (1973), *On The Beach* (1974) and *Tonight's The Night* (1975, recorded in 1973). His next album *Zuma* (1975) featured one of Young's most celebrated songs, 'Cortez The Killer'. 1978's *Rust Never Sleeps* represented a positive reaction to punk, befitting an artist who has never allowed himself to become complacent.

ZZ Top

(Vocal/instrumental group, 1969–present)

A visually distinctive Texan trio comprising Billy Gibbons (vocals, guitar), Dusty Hill (bass, vocals) and Frank Beard (drums), ZZ Top honed their southern boogie through constant gigging. Supporting The Rolling Stones brought them to a wider audience and the third album *Tres Hombres* (1973) was the band's commercial breakthrough. They went on to experience million-selling success with 1983's *Eliminator* and the singles 'Gimme All Your Lovin'', 'Sharp Dressed Man' and 'Legs'.

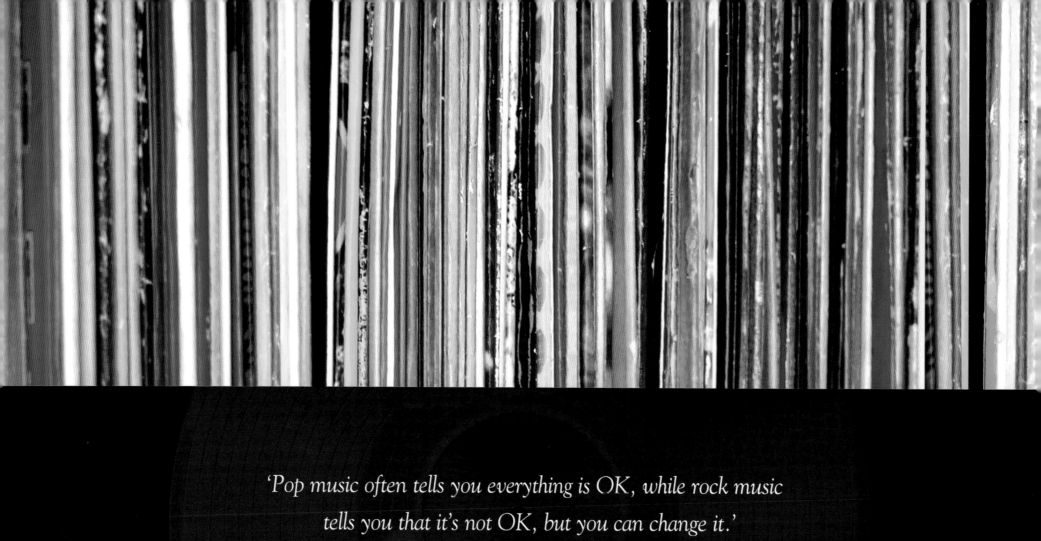

'Pop music often tells you everything is OK, while rock music tells you that it's not OK, but you can change it.'

Bono, U2

The Eighties

The Eighties: ELECTRIC VIBES & VISUALS

This was a decade when the impact of dance culture on rock and vice versa sometimes led to exciting results: it opened with 'Thriller' and closed with the Madchester scene of Happy Mondays.

The synthesizer was the decade's dominant instrument, many groups replacing their guitars with them. David Bowie was the single main influence on the decade's visual style, his 1980 hit 'Fashion' becoming something of an anthem.

Essential Recordings

- 1982 Michael Jackson: *Thriller*
- 1983 The Police: *Every Breath You Take*
- 1984 Prince: *Purple Rain*
- 1986 Bon Jovi: *Slippery When Wet*
- 1987 U2: *The Joshua Tree*
- 1989 Madonna: *Like A Prayer*

A New Attitude

The previous decade had gone out with a bang in the spitting, snarling shape of punk. In the 1980s, musicians took the energy of punk and lost the attitude, resulting in 'new wave', a highly marketable proposition, which, along with the new romantics, dominated the early days of the decade.

The biggest single promoter of 1980s music was MTV (Music Television), which first broadcast its videos in the States in 1981. It would take until the end of the decade for satellite television to reach Britain, but by that time it had proved itself a star-maker of the highest order.

In 1982 Michael Jackson created the soundtrack for the 1980s dance floor in the shape of the 110 million-selling *Thriller*. 'Jacko' was also the first black artist to break big on MTV, thanks to his innovative videos.

Jackson's female counterpart Madonna made an indelible mark on both sides of the Atlantic, and few female performers would remain untouched by her influence.

Political Awareness

The 1980s was the decade when rock rediscovered its conscience. Boomtown Rat Bob Geldof followed up 1984's charity single 'Do They Know It's Christmas?' with simultaneous all-star concerts at Wembley Stadium and JFK Stadium, Philadelphia. Fifteen-minute mini-sets were the order of the day, with Queen stealing the show.

Madonna

Rock stars recording Band Aid single

As the decade rolled on, 'conscience rock' did its bit for many good causes, while the Nelson Mandela 70th Birthday Tribute Concert in 1988 was an awareness-raising exercise that hastened the release of the future South African president.

In With The New

The compact disc arrived in Europe in 1983 and, by the end of the decade, the traditional vinyl record was on its way out. Although initially derided as a 'yuppie' status symbol, the handy five-inch format became ubiquitous as the decade continued.

Heavy rock enjoyed boosts at the beginning and the end of the decade. The first flowering came in the shape of the so-called New Wave of British Heavy Metal (NWOBHM), which spawned the likes of Saxon, Iron Maiden and Motörhead. By the end of the decade the US answer to NWOBHM had materialized, resulting in mammoth sales for the likes of ultimate 'hair band' Bon Jovi. From Britain, Def Leppard managed to catch the coat-tails of the movement to enjoy Stateside success that continues today.

With legwarmers, 'Frankie Says' T-shirts and Spandau Ballet's kilts, the 1980s was the decade when popular music dressed to impress. It was also the decade when video killed the radio star: from now on, you would have to look the part as well as sound it.

'I came here to play music, and I didn't really realize the full extent and magnitude of what it is all about. Now I'm here. It's the greatest event ever.' **Ozzy Osbourne on Live Aid**

Headline Acts

The Beastie Boys

(Vocal/rap/instrumental group, 1981–present)

The Beastie Boys – Michael 'Mike D' Diamond, Adam 'MCA' Yauch and Adam 'King Ad-Rock' Horovitz – began life as a New York hardcore punk band, but under the auspices of producer Rick Rubin became the first important white rap act. Debut *Licensed To Ill* (1986) was a good-time rap-metal crossover, which spawned the hit singles '(You Gotta) Fight For Your Right (To Party!)', 'No Sleep Till Brooklyn' and 'She's On It'. These bratty anthems and the band's over-the-top stage show caused as much controversy as first-wave punk. *Licensed…* was the first No. 1 rap album in the US. Disputes with Rubin led to a hiatus. The unexpectedly diverse and even thoughtful *Paul's Boutique* arrived in 1989. Equally interesting collections arrived at fairly lengthy intervals: the funky *Check Your Head* (1992), *Ill Communication* (1994), and double Grammy-winning *Hello Nasty* (1998). Over 25 years, they stretched rap's boundaries and produced some of the wittiest music around.

Bon Jovi

(Vocal/instrumental group, 1983–present)

Led by singer Jon Bon Jovi (born John Francis Bongiovi) and guitarist Richie Sambora, Bon Jovi were America's leading hard rock band in the 1980s. The band includes keyboard player David Bryan, bassist Alec John Such and drummer Tico Torres.

The Beastie Boys

The eponymous *Bon Jovi* (1984) stalled just outside the US Top 40 but *7800 Fahrenheit* (1985) made the UK Top 30 following a British tour. *Slippery When Wet* (1986) stormed to the top of the US charts, propelled by two No. 1 singles – 'You Give Love A Bad Name' and 'Livin' On A Prayer'.

The band returned undiminished after two hiatuses in 1990–91 and 1997–99. *Keep The Faith* (1992) updated their sound and *Crush* (2000) showed that another lay-off had not damaged their status. Such then left, while Sambora has battled substance abuse problems.

No longer innovators, Bon Jovi nevertheless retain their popularity with pop and rock fans, male and female.

Kate Bush

(Singer/songwriter, piano b. 1958)

Catherine 'Kate' Bush CBE was the first female singer to top the UK charts with a self-penned song ('Wuthering Heights', 1978). She is a versatile and sometimes surreal songwriter whose work involves adventurous sound experimentation. The subject matter of her songs has embraced everything from Emily Brontë's characters to controversial psychoanalyst Wilhelm Reich ('Cloudbusting', 1985). Often perceived as a perfectionist (a charge she denies), she has frequently stood her ground against record-company influence and won. She rarely tours. Pink Floyd's David Gilmour has long championed her music – she sang the part of the doctor in a 2002 live performance of 'Comfortably Numb' – and collaborated with Peter Gabriel in the 1980s on two songs: 'Games Without Frontiers' and 'Don't Give Up'. Bush has been cited as a major influence by other female singer/songwriters including Björk, K.T. Tunstall, Lily Allen, Courtney Love and P.J. Harvey.

Nick Cave

(Singer/songwriter b. 1957)

Nick Cave (vocals) began his fascinating career in Boys Next Door, who became The Birthday Party: Mick Harvey (guitar), Tracy Pew (bass), Phil Calvert (drums). A gothic, blues punk band of fearsome intensity, showcasing Cave's brutal, Captain Beefheart-style lyrics, they released three albums, 1981's *Prayers On Fire* being the pick. 1982's *Junkyard* is the sound of the band falling apart.

Nick Cave

Cave regrouped, retaining Mick Harvey and adding guitarist Blixa Bargeld to form the slightly less deranged Bad Seeds. Their highly influential mixture of corrupted lounge music, gothic gospel and misanthropic post-punk balladry is displayed on many fine albums, including *From Her To Eternity* (1984), *Henry's Dream* (1992), *Murder Ballads* (1996; Kylie Minogue and P.J. Harvey guest), and the very witty *Abattoir Blues/Lyre Of Orpheus* (2004). Cave is an important figure, a Leonard Cohen for Generation X.

The Cure

(Vocal/instrumental group, 1976–present)

Influential UK post-punk outfit led by wild-haired Robert Smith (vocals, guitar). Their debut album *Three Imaginary Boys* (1979) preceded the much darker *Seventeen Seconds* (1980), *Faith* (1981) and *Pornography* (1982). 'Let's Go To Bed' showed Smith's quirky pop sensibility, while 'Just Like Heaven', 'Lovesong' and 'Friday I'm in Love' gave them substantial hit success in America. Often hailed as fathers of goth, they inspired many on the alternative music scene.

Def Leppard

(Vocal/instrumental group, 1977–present)

The band appropriately formed in Sheffield, erstwhile home of the British steel industry. Their fresh brand of poppy heavy metal, led by Joe Elliott (vocals) and Pete Willis (lead guitar), soon won them fans. An early B-side 'Hello America' hinted at their ambitions. Debut album *On Through The Night* (1980) just missed the US Top 50, but with 1983's *Pyromania* they became giants of the genre, hitting the stateside No. 2. Drummer Rick Allen lost an arm in a car accident, but adapted his kit, and 1987's *Hysteria* made US No. 1, and UK No. 2. Guitarist Steve Clark died from drink and drugs in 1991, but once again the band returned, topping the charts with *Adrenalize* (1992). Since these heady days – replete with smashes such as 'Love Bites' and 'Let's Get Rocked' – they have modernized successfully on *Slang* (1996), *Euphoria* (1999) and *X* (2002). Their pioneering, catchy pop rock still draws crowds.

Depeche Mode

(Vocal/instrumental group, 1976–present)

The band was formed by Essex schoolboys Vince Clarke (keyboards), Martin Gore (vocals, guitar, keyboards), Andy Fletcher (keyboards) and singer Dave Gahan. New label Mute took a punt on their melancholic but hooky synth-pop and were rewarded with the Top 10 album *Speak And Spell* (1981) and classic dance track 'Just Can't Get Enough'. Clarke departed to create Erasure, and Gore assumed songwriting duties, racking up hits that combined Gahan's world-weary delivery with a riffy, industrial-lite appeal – 'Everything Counts', 'People Are People' (their first US hit) and 'Master And Servant'. Deeply depressive collections such as *Some Great Reward* (1984), *Black Celebration* (1986) and *Music For The Masses* (1987) cemented their US reputation, while 1990's *Violator* and its premier single 'Personal Jesus' marked a move to a more guitar-oriented sound. Bands such as Nine Inch Nails paid homage. Gahan suffered drug-related problems in the 1990s, but varied outings such as *Ultra* (1997) and *Exciter* (2001) proved the band had plenty of life left.

Dire Straits

(Vocal/instrumental group, 1977–95)

Led by guitarist Mark Knopfler with brother David (guitar), John Illsley (bass) and Pick Withers (drums), Dire Straits went from playing the London pub circuit to a US hit album. Knopfler's inventive, plectrum-free guitar playing, street-poet lyrics and fine pop rock tunesmithery combined to launch their huge career. Their debut single, 'Sultans Of Swing', was a punchy, likeable helping of Dylanesque roots rock. *Communique* (1979) and *Love Over Gold* (1982) paved the way for the multiple-platinum *Brothers In Arms* (1985). 'Money For Nothing' from that selection satirized the very business they were in. Only one studio album, 1991's slightly disappointing *On Every Street,* followed, and Knopfler embarked on a solo career that included soundtrack composition. Dire Straits will be remembered as an intelligent but accessible band who could run the gamut from the borderline experimental (the intro to 'Private Investigations', 1982) to the chug-a-long pop rock of 'Walk Of Life' (1985).

Mark Knopfler of Dire Straits

Eurythmics

Duran Duran

(Vocal/instrumental group, 1978–present)

The most glamorous of the new romantic bands, Birmingham's Duran Duran (named after the evil scientist in the movie *Barbarella*) looked very good in the ambitious videos that accompanied their many Top 10 hits. These included 'Girls On Film' (1981), 'Hungry Like The Wolf', 'Save A Prayer' and 'Rio' (all 1982), 'The Reflex' and 'Wild Boys' (1984): a mixture of sexually charged, up-tempo pop and beguiling ballads, which played perfectly to the hedonism of the decade. The albums combined these approaches to varying effect, with 1982's *Rio* (which broke the band in America in 1983), probably the best of the bunch. In 1985, Simon Le Bon (vocals), Nick Rhodes (keyboards) and Roger Taylor (drums) worked on side project Arcadia, while the Taylors, Andy (guitar) and John (bass), joined The Power Station. After these excursions some of the magic seemed to have gone, excepting 1993's *The Wedding Album*, which yielded the smash 'Ordinary World'.

Eurythmics

(Vocal/instrumental group, 1980–90, 1999–2005)

Dave Stewart (keyboards, guitars) and Annie Lennox (vocals) were Eurythmics. In 1983, the title track of *Sweet Dreams (Are Made Of This)* went to No. 1 in America. The synth-powered pop noir of 'Who's That Girl' was followed by the joyous, tropical-tinged 'Right By Your Side', proving their adaptability and intelligence. (Lennox's versatile, soulful voice is almost unparalleled in modern pop.) Another 1983 album, *Touch*, yielded the yearning 'Here Comes The Rain Again'. On *Be Yourself Tonight* (1985) their bluesier side emerged, with hit singles such as 'Would I Lie To You?' and the wonderful 'Sisters Are Doin' It For Themselves' with Aretha Franklin. The album's beautiful 'There Must Be An Angel' became their only UK No. 1. Their truly great albums behind them, they still released great singles in 'Missionary Man' (1986) and 'I Need A Man' (1988) before solo careers beckoned.

Foreigner

(Vocal/instrumental group, 1976–present)

These AOR giants established themselves in 1977 with their eponymous debut album and single 'Feels Like The First Time', which both reached No. 4 in the US. The band was founded by Englishman Mick Jones (guitar) with Lou Gramm's dramatic tenor vocals to the fore. The original line-up was completed by Ian McDonald (guitar, keyboards), Al Greenwood (keyboards, replaced by Rick Wills, 1979), Ed Gagliardi (bass) and Dennis Elliott (drums). Further hits such as 'Cold As Ice' and 'Double Vision' piled up in America, then 1981's *4* attained the UK Top 5. Their monster smash, the mother of all power ballads 'I Want To Know What Love Is' arrived in 1984. But Gramm was getting restless; he cut a solo album and then left officially. Johnny Edwards filled his shoes, but it was clear that the band's days as the US's top melodic rock outfit were over, even when Gramm returned in the mid-1990s; he left again in 2003.

Frankie Goes To Hollywood

(Vocal/instrumental group, 1980–87)

Fronted by the charismatic Holly Johnson, FGTH – Paul Rutherford (vocals), Peter Gill (drums), Mark O'Toole (bass) and Brian Nash (guitar) – hit Britain with three consecutive No. 1s: the exciting, synthesized funk pop of 1983's 'Relax' (banned by the BBC) and 'Two Tribes' – both precursors of house music – and the huge ballad 'The Power Of Love', all inventively produced by Trevor Horn. The title track of *Welcome To The Pleasure Dome* (1984) only reached No. 2. After a second album, named after their hometown, *Liverpool* (1986), Johnson went solo.

Foreigner

Axl Rose of Guns N' Roses

Peter Gabriel

(Singer/songwriter, b. 1950)

Gabriel left Genesis in 1975. His first solo album produced the intriguing hit 'Solsbury Hill', telling of that departure. In 1980, the avant-pop of 'Games Without Frontiers' began a run of accessible art rock albums and singles including the political 'Biko', 1982's *Peter Gabriel* (*Security* in the US), and 1986's triumphant world-music influenced *So* and its mega-hit 'Sledgehammer'. Gabriel now spends much of his time on his influential world-music label, Real World.

Guns N' Roses

(Vocal/instrumental group, 1985–present)

Axl Rose (b. William Bailey, vocals) and Izzy Stradlin (b. Jeffrey Isbell, guitar) were joined by Slash (b. Saul Hudson, guitar), Duff McKagan (bass) and Steve Adler (drums) to form a band that gave the heavy rock scene a mighty shaking. Signed to Geffen – after the 1986 EP *Live ?1*@ Like A Suicide* had attracted industry interest – their debut album *Appetite For Destruction* (1987) combined the attack of AC/DC with a punk aesthetic and powerful lyrics about the underbelly of LA. It went to the US No. 1 spot, as did 'Sweet Child O' Mine'. The next few years saw much debauchery; the departure of Adler; the US Top 5 ballad 'Patience'; and the releases of the massive-selling *Use Your Illusion I* and *II* (1991). Stradlin also jumped ship; as, in 1995, did Slash, to form Slash's Snakepit and then Velvet Revolver. Rose keeps the name of the band alive.

The Happy Mondays

(Vocal/instrumental group, 1980–93, 1999, 2004–10, 2012–present)

Led by vocalist Shaun Ryder, the band were at the forefront of the 'Madchester' scene. They appropriated licks from psychedelia, soul and hip-hop to come up with a danceable brand of rock that reached its apotheosis on 1990's *Pills 'n' Thrills And Bellyaches*, which included UK Top 5s 'Step On' and 'Kinky Afro'. The chaotic, drug-addled nature of the band meant the hits diminished, and when the Factory label subsided, Ryder moved on to form Black Grape.

INXS

(Vocal/instrumental group, 1977–2012)

Led by the charismatic Michael Hutchence (vocals), the band broke into the American market with *Shabooh Shoobah* (1982). 1985's *Listen Like Thieves* consolidated their position, while *Kick* (1987) and 'Need You

Tonight' – No. 1 in America and No. 2 in the UK – confirmed their impact. Hutchence's death in 1997 came by his own hand. Although INXS continued sporadically with different frontmen, they disbanded permanently in 2012.

Iron Maiden

(Vocal/instrumental group, 1975–present)

Original lead vocalist Paul Di'Anno led this East London heavy metal outfit to No. 4 on the UK chart in 1980 with their self-titled debut. New singer Bruce Dickinson went three places better with 1982's *The Number Of The Beast.* The band soon became Britain's top metal group, with their hard rocking, if slightly tongue-in-cheek, approach. Steve Harris (bass, vocals), Dave Murray (guitar), Adrian Smith (guitar) and Nicko McBrain (drums) are the most enduring members, though both Dickinson and Smith left and returned. Between 1985 and 1995 the band's singles and albums were rarely out of the Top 10 in the UK, or Top 20 in the US. Particular highlights include the 1988 concept album *Seventh Son Of A Seventh Son*, and the bullet-spitting rock of 1990's *No Prayer For The Dying*, which spawned the band's only UK No. 1 single 'Bring Your Daughter… To The Slaughter'.

Michael Hutchence of INXS

Iron Maiden

Michael Jackson

(Singer 1958–2009)

Michael Jackson, the 'King of Pop', was the biggest star of the 1980s following the success of *Thriller,* which remains the world's best-selling album with sales of more than 110 million.

The youngest of The Jackson Five, Jackson signed a solo contract with Motown Records in 1971. 'Got To Be There' and 'Rockin' Robin' reached the Top 5; 'Ben' topped the charts. His first album with producer Quincy Jones was *Off The Wall* (1979). It won two Grammy Awards in 1981.

Thriller (1982) spawned an unprecedented seven US Top 10 singles including 'Billie Jean' and 'Beat It'. It won eight Grammy Awards in 1984 and stayed at No. 1 in America for 37 weeks – it was still in the charts 21 months later. The mini-epic video for 'Thriller' ensured Jackson became the first black artist to get regular exposure on MTV.

Classic Recordings

1979 *Off The Wall, Don't Stop 'Til You Get Enough*
1982 *Thriller*
1983 *Billie Jean, Beat It*
1987 *Bad, I Just Can't Stop Loving You, Bad*
1988 *Smooth Criminal*
1991 *Black Or White*
1995 *You Are Not Alone*

Thriller was an impossible album to follow but *Bad* (1987) sold 22 million copies and produced five US No. 1 singles including 'Man In The Mirror'. It was the last album Jackson made with Jones.

Dangerous (1991), co-produced by Teddy Riley, topped the US charts for four weeks and 'Black Or White' reached No. 1. The *Dangerous* world tour ended prematurely in 1993 when he was engulfed in scandal involving child abuse allegations. These were settled out of court but caused lasting damage to his reputation.

Invincible (2001) was Jackson's first album of all-new material since *Dangerous* and debuted at No. 1 in the US, selling over 11 million worldwide.

But controversy was never far away. In 2005 he faced more child abuse allegations. He was acquitted, and his death in June 2009 on the eve of a comeback tour saw him deified by millions of followers.

'He was like a sponge. Michael showed a curiosity for everything. It was unbelievable in someone so young. I appreciated watching it work.'

Quincy Jones

Billy Joel

(Singer/songwriter, b. 1949)

New Yorker William Martin Joel released his first solo album in 1972, and broke into the US Top 30 with his second set, *Piano Man* in 1975. 'Just The Way You Are' became his first major hit in 1977. 1980's chart-topping *Glass Houses* gave him his first No. 1, the infectious 'It's Still Rock'n'Roll To Me'. 1983's *Innocent Man* generated three US Top 10 singles – the title track, 'Uptown Girl' and 'Tell Her About It'. Joel now works in the classical world.

Judas Priest

(Vocal/instrumental group, 1969–present)

This Birmingham heavy metal outfit, led by vocalist Rob Halford, first charted with *Sin After Sin* in 1977. *British Steel* (1980) consolidated their position as one of the leading bands in the New Wave of British Heavy Metal. Their lyrics littered with Satanic imagery, the band were unsuccessfully sued in 1985 by parents of two of the band's fans who committed suicide. Storming albums such as *Screaming For Vengeance* (1982) were an acknowledged influence on Metallica and others.

Judas Priest

Madonna

Madness
(Vocal/instrumental group, 1976–present)

This London band – Graham 'Suggs' McPherson and Chas Smash (both vocals), Dan Woodgate (drums), Mark Bedford (bass), Mike Barson (keyboards), Chris Foreman (guitar) and Lee Thompson (saxophone) – only managed one US hit, 1983's 'Our House', but inspired the American ska-punkers of the 1990s. 1979's *One Step Beyond* was a cornerstone of the ska revival, but Madness soon developed a broader pop-oriented sensibility. An influence on the likes of Blur and Supergrass, their use of videos was trailblazing. Highlights include 'Embarrassment' (1979), 'House Of Fun' (1982) and 'The Sun And The Rain' (1983).

Madonna
(Singer/songwriter, b. Madonna Louise Ciccone 1958)

The most successful female recording artist of all time, Madonna began her recording career in 1982 when she signed to Sire Records.

Like A Virgin (1984) and its title track established Madonna as an international star. It was produced by Nile Rodgers (of Chic fame). Her first UK No. 1 single 'Into The Groove' (1985) was followed by blockbuster *True Blue* in 1986 featuring 'Papa Don't Preach', 'Open Your Heart' and 'La Isla Bonita'.

Madonna starred in the 1987 film *Who's That Girl* and the soundtrack album featured four of her songs. Her next album, *Like a Prayer* (1989), courted controversy, and valuable publicity, over its use of religious imagery. *The Immaculate Collection* (1990) became one of the best-selling greatest hits compilations ever, with many of its tracks remixed and edited.

Erotica (1992), an album themed around sexuality, was largely overshadowed by *Sex*, a book that featured soft-core photography and Madonna's explicit prose. In 1996, she played the title role in the film adaptation of the Andrew Lloyd Webber/Tim Rice musical *Evita*.

She worked with British musician/producer William Orbit on *Ray Of Light* (1998). The album blended pop with electronica, ambient trance and quasi-psychedelia. Further collaborations with Orbit followed on *Music* (2000).

2003's *American Life* was mired in controversy when, during the prelude to the second Iraq war, the video for the title track was criticized as unpatriotic; the album, a blend of acoustic and techno, suffered commercially.

Megadeth

Confessions On A Dance Floor (2005) returned Madonna to straightforward dance music, but her personal life, including marriage to and divorce from film director Guy Ritchie, dalliance with the Kabbalah religious sect and the attempted adoption of sundry African children, has of late attracted more attention than her recorded output. She reunited with William Orbit (among others) for 2012's US chart-topping *MDNA*.

Meat Loaf

(Vocals, b. 1947)

Born Marvin Lee Aday in Dallas, Texas, Meat Loaf had a musical theatre as well as a rock'n'roll background (he starred in *The Rocky Horror Picture Show*). This was apparent on the camp but hugely appealing excess of breakthrough album *Bat Out Of Hell* in 1977, written by Jim Steinman and produced by Todd Rundgren. The live shows supporting the album have attained mythic status, with Meat Loaf's good-naturedly melodramatic delivery and massive stature making him an unlikely rock icon. Its successor, *Dead Ringer* (1981), did even better in the UK, topping the charts, with 'Dead Ringer For Love' – featuring Cher as co-vocalist – also a hit. Meat Loaf released several pot-boiling collections before reuniting with Steinman for *Bat Out Of Hell II: Back Into Hell* (1993), which was a transatlantic No. 1, as was its main single 'I'd Do Anything For Love (But I Won't Do That)'.

Megadeth

(Vocal/instrumental group, 1983–present)

Ex-Metallica guitarist Dave Mustaine hardened and sped up his erstwhile band's already ferocious thrash metal. His pessimistic, politicized lyrics drive the likes of *Peace Sells … But Who's Buying?* (1986) and his best album so far *Rust In Peace* (1990), matching his former employers' impact in the process. After an attempt to go more mainstream the band – essentially Mustaine with hired hands – returned to form with *The System Has Failed* (2004), featuring original guitarist Chris Poland.

George Michael

George Michael

(Singer/songwriter, b. 1963)

Born Georgios Panayiotou of North London, Greek-Cypriot heritage, Michael served a very public initiation with teeny-boppers Wham!. In the mid-1980s he released a pair of solo singles, 'Careless Whisper' and 'A Different Corner', dissolving Wham! in 1986. He re-emerged in 1987 with the pristine adult pop of *Faith*, which hooked the American market. A series of singles, including 'Father Figure', 'One More Try' and 'Monkey', performed better in the US than the UK. 1990's *Listen Without Prejudice Vol 1* was an altogether darker affair, which heralded a battle with record label Sony. The dispute was resolved in 1995, clearing the way for the introspective *Older* (1996), which nevertheless furnished several hit singles, including 'Fastlove' and 'Jesus To A Child'. In 2006, Michael started his first tour in 15 years, a massive, worldwide undertaking that saw him perform in 41 countries to two million fans. It was accompanied by the compilation *Twenty Five*.

Motley Crüe

(Vocal/instrumental group, 1980–present)

Vince Neil (vocals), Mick Mars (guitar), Nikki Sixx (bass) and Tommy Lee (drums) became the world's most notorious heavy metal band, as much for their off-record excesses as for their music. They released their crude but effective glam metal debut *Too Fast For Love* in 1981. Over the years, they became technically more adept, and the production got slicker, but their lyrical subject matter (sex and drugs and rock'n'roll) remained the same. *Shout At The Devil* (1983) became their American Top 20 debut. *Theatre Of Pain* (1985) and *Girls Girls Girls* (1987) kept the ball rolling and *Dr. Feelgood* (1989) registered their first No. 1 (No. 4 in the UK). Guns N' Roses, obviously influenced by The Crüe, had emerged by this time, and a feud erupted between the two bands. Neil left in 1992, returning in 1996 for more ever-so-slightly toned-down mayhem.

Motörhead

(Vocal/instrumental group, 1975–present)

The seemingly indestructible Lemmy Kilmister (vocals, bass) was a former member of Hawkwind, and a vicar's son. Motörhead are named after a Hawkwind song he penned. The line-up settled in the late 1970s with 'Fast' Eddie Clarke (guitar) and Phil 'Filthy Animal' Taylor (drums). The title track of 1980's *Ace Of Spades* was a UK hit, and became the blueprint for the band's sound for the next quarter of a century: ear-shatteringly loud guitar, chordal bass and Kilmister's gruff vocals shouted over the top. Their gigs are legendary, often featuring a life-size replica of a German bomber. The live experience was captured on a UK No. 1 from 1981 *No Sleep 'Til Hammersmith* (book-ended in 1988 by *No Sleep At All*). Personnel changes in bass and drum departments did not much alter their sound, which was highly influential on the thrash and nu-metal scenes.

Tom Petty

(Singer/songwriter, b. 1950)

Petty, born in Gainsville, Florida, formed his long-time backing band The Heartbreakers from Mike Campbell (guitar), Benmont Tench (keyboards), Ron Blair (bass) and Stan Lynch (drums). An eponymous album in 1977 was a hard-hitting brand of country rock, with plenty of modern attack, rootsy authenticity and good tunes. The UK was impressed, but it was not until 1979's *Damn The Torpedoes* that the US took a native son (and another 'new Dylan') to its breast. Alongside Springsteen, Petty helped revitalize the reputation of intelligent blue-collar rock, while tapping into its folkier heritage. They scored a couple of big US singles in 'Refugee' (1979) and 'Don't Do Me Like That' (1980). In 1988, Petty wound up the band, working with Bob Dylan, Roy Orbison and George Harrison in The Traveling Wilburys. An excellent solo album, *Full Moon Fever,* resulted in 1989, before The Heartbreakers reformed: still one of America's most consistent bands behind a consistently good songwriter.

The Pixies

(Vocal/instrumental group, 1986–93, 2004–present)

One of the most important alternative rock bands ever came together in Boston with Charles Thompson IV, who styled himself Black Francis (vocals, guitar), Joey Santiago (guitar), Kim Deal (bass, vocals), and Dave Lovering (drums). Lyrically, Thompson explored religion, weird sex and sci-fi, singing with a preternaturally forceful yelp. The words were fitted to an eclectic array of styles. Punk, surf, pop, hardcore and Spanish elements all collided on a succession of superb albums: the raging *Surfer Rosa* (1988), 1989's *Doolittle* (by far the poppiest), *Bossanova* (1990) and *Trompe Le Monde* (1991). Their stop-start dynamics were a strong influence on Nirvana. Their combination of melody and abrasiveness, and Santiago's skewed guitar heroics, were also adopted by many indie rockers. Ultimately, Deal wanted more of her songs used. Frank Black, as he soon became in his solo career, refused. She formed The Breeders. The Pixies reunited to play ecstatically received gigs in 2004.

Tom Petty

The Police

The Police

(Vocal/instrumental group, 1977–84, 2007–08)

One of the 1980s' most successful reggae-influenced British bands featuring Sting (Gordon Sumner – vocals/bass), Andy Summers (guitar) and Stewart Copeland (drums), whose debut album *Outlandos d'Amour* (1978) spawned three major singles in 'Roxanne', 'Can't Stand Losing You' and 'So Lonely'.

Reggatta De Blanc (1979) and *Zenyatta Mondatta* (1980) were highly successful follow-ups, along with the singles from them: 'Message In A Bottle', 'Walking On The Moon' and 'Don't Stand So Close To Me'.

'Invisible Sun' and 'Every Little Thing She Does Is Magic' were singles from *Ghost In The Machine* (1981), and their final album was *Synchronicity* (1983), from which UK chart topper 'Every Breath You Take' was taken.

After The Police folded in 1984 the three went their own ways, Sting enjoying solo success with *Dream Of The Blue Turtles* (1985) and *Ten Summoner's Tales* (1993). He has also been heavily involved in political and environmental campaigning. The Police reunited for a world tour in 2007-08.

The Pretenders

(Vocal/instrumental group, 1978–present)

Ohio-born, British-based Chrissie Hynde's tough, tuneful voice has established her as an iconic female rocker. 'Brass In Pocket' was a UK No. 1 in 1979, and in America the following year. Hynde and drummer Martin Chambers overcame the loss of original members James Honeyman-Scott and Pete Farndon to drugs in 1982 and 1983. *Pretenders II* (1981) and *Learning To Crawl* (1984) charted highly, and in 1986 'Don't Get Me Wrong' went Top 10.

Prince

(Singer, multi-instrumentalist, songwriter b. Prince Rogers Nelson, 1958)

The most innovative, enigmatic and controversial black rock star since Jimi Hendrix, his debut, *For You* (1978), was self-written and self-played, a blend of R&B, rock and pop with controversial titles like 'Soft And Wet'. Follow-up *Prince* (1979) peaked just outside the US Top 20, while for *Controversy* (1981) he refined his adult-oriented funk. His breakthrough came with the harder-rocking double album *1999* (1982), which hit the US charts on the back of three Top 10 singles: 'Little Red Corvette', 'Delirious' and the title track.

Purple Rain (1984) launched Prince to superstardom, topping the US charts for 24 weeks. It featured two US No. 1 hits – 'When Doves Cry' and 'Let's Go Crazy'. In 1985, he won two Grammies and an Oscar and released *Around The World In A Day* (1985), which topped the US charts for three weeks and made the UK Top 5. *Parade* (1986), his eighth album in as many years, went Top 5 in the US and UK and featured songs from his second movie, *Under The Cherry Moon*, including 'Kiss'. There followed a succession of critically acclaimed hit albums, including *Sign 'O' The Times* (1987), *Lovesexy* (1988), *Batman* (1989), the soundtrack to the year's movie blockbuster, and *Graffiti Bridge* (1990).

For *Symbol* (1992), Prince created his own hieroglyph, amalgamating the male and female symbols, and scored his fourth UK No. 1 (US No. 6). He then changed his name to the unpronounceable symbol and became embroiled in a contractual dispute over his next album.

The Minneapolis musician's contract with Warner Bros ended, appropriately enough, with *Chaos And Disorder* (1996), a US Top 30 and UK Top 20 album. But once independent, he made little effort to court commercial success until the focused *Musicology* (2004).

Public Image Limited
(Vocal/instrumental group, 1978–93, 2009–present)

Johnny Rotten reinvented himself after The Sex Pistols as John Lydon. With Keith Levene (guitar, drums) and Jah Wobble (bass), PiL released an eponymous debut album in 1978. Their second collection, 1979's *Metal Box*, was released as *Second Edition* (1980) in the US, having made the UK Top 20. 'This Is Not A Love Song' and 'Rise' were UK hits in 1985 and 1986. The band re-formed in 2009.

Run DMC
(Rap group, 1982–2002)

Pioneers of hip-hop, Run was born Joseph Simmons; DMC was Darryl McDaniel; with Jam Master Jay (b. Jason Mizell) on the decks. Their big, simple beats were heard on the eponymous debut (1983) and *King Of Rock* (1985), and as part of the first and best rock-rap crossover 'Walk This Way' with Aerosmith. Run eventually translated his socially conscious raps into a Christian ministry. 'It's Like That' topped the UK chart in 1998, but their story ended in tragedy with the shooting of Jay in 2002.

Joe Satriani
(Guitar, b. 1956)

Satriani was an influential teacher – students include Steve Vai, Kirk Hammett of Metallica and Primus's Larry LaLonde – before becoming a recording artist in his late 20s. He is not simply a stunt-guitarist, even though some of his playing on his debut *Surfing With The Alien* (1987) is jaw-dropping. It reached the US Top 30 and inspired a generation of players. He mixes a plethora of styles from rock'n'roll workouts to lyrical ballads via jazz and funk odysseys. He added passable vocals to *Flying In A Blue Dream* (1989). 1992's *The Extremist* went to a surprising No. 13 in the UK, after nu-metal guitarists started to sing his praises. After a short spell with Deep Purple he released an entertaining live set with former pupil Vai and fellow axe-man Eric Johnson, entitled *G3 In Concert* (1997). Ever open-minded, he even experimented with electronica on *Engines Of Creation* (2001).

Simple Minds
(Vocal/instrumental group, 1977–present)

Formerly known as Johnny and The Self-Abusers, Glaswegians Jim Kerr (vocals), Charlie Burchill (guitar), Derek Forbes (bass), Mick McNeil (keyboards) and Brian McGee (drums) took on board the experimentations of Krautrock and Brian Eno for their second album *Real To Real Cacophony* (1979). They gently sloughed off their weirder tendencies over their next two albums, before 1982's *New Gold Dream (81-82-83-84)* chimed with the era's love of melodic, but mildly arty synth-pop. The album went to No. 3 and housed their first hits 'Promised You A Miracle' and 'Glittering Prize'. It also gained them a foothold in America, which they exploited with 1984's *Sparkle In The Rain* and US chart-topper 'Don't You (Forget About Me)'. *Once Upon A Time* (1985) kept up the momentum, as they vied with U2 as the world's No. 1 stadium rock band; but by the early 1990s Jim Kerr's anthemic pop was beginning to date.

Jim Kerr of Simple Minds

The Smiths

The Smiths
(Vocal/instrumental group, 1982–87)

Manchester's finest coalesced around the songwriting pair of former journalist Stephen Patrick Morrissey (vocals) and Johnny Marr (guitar). Andy Rourke (bass) and Mike Joyce (drums) completed a team who became the darlings of bed-sit melancholics everywhere, and exerted a huge influence on indie rock over the following decades. Their mesmerizing blend of 1960s beat music and new wave artiness was driven by Marr's ringing, inventive guitar, topped off by Morrissey's idiosyncratic wail and clever, often drily humorous lyrics. In 1984, 'What Difference Does It Make?' went Top 20 and their self-titled debut album waltzed to No. 2. 1985's *Meat Is Murder* went one better, while *The Queen Is Dead* from the following year broke America. The shimmering power of 'How Soon Is Now' represents one of the best singles of the decade. Tensions between Morrissey and Marr grew and a split in 1987 became inevitable. Both went on to strong solo careers.

Sonic Youth
(Vocal/instrumental group, 1981–present)

Starting life as avant-garde noise merchants, Thurston Moore (vocals, guitar), Kim Gordon (bass, vocals), Lee Ranaldo (guitar, vocals) and a variety of drummers, including Steve Shelley, have been at the centre of New York's alternative music scene ever since, influencing indie rock immeasurably. Highlights include the striking art rock of 1987's *Sister;* the almost conventional *Goo* (1990); their Madonna covers side project, Ciccone Youth; and a typically genre-defying collaboration with Chuck D of Public Enemy.

Talking Heads
(Vocal/instrumental group, 1975–91)

David Byrne (vocals), Tina Weymouth (vocals) and Chris Frantz (drums) formed Talking Heads at art school and were signed after performances at New York's famed CBGB. Jerry Harrison (guitar, keyboards) joined soon after. Their 1977 debut album *Talking Heads '77* established their nervy, funky style, with Byrne's cryptic lyrics. Brian Eno became their producer with *More Songs About Buildings And Food* (1978). *Fear Of Music* (1979) broadened their palate with African sounds, while *Remain In Light* (1980) yielded the UK hit 'Once In A Lifetime'. Live album *Stop Making Sense* (1984), with its wonderful Jonathan Demme-directed film, set new standards in the field. After 1985's *Little Creatures*, the band, particularly Byrne, seemed distracted by solo projects (Frantz and Weymouth with Tom Tom Club, Byrne with his world music label Luaka Bop) and the end was inevitable. Giants of new wave, and immeasurably influential, they made art rock palatable to the mainstream.

U2

(Vocal/instrumental group, 1978–present)

One of the world's most successful rock groups, Ireland's U2 consists of Bono (b. Paul Hewson, vocals), The Edge (b. David Evans, guitar), Adam Clayton (bass) and Larry Mullen Jr. (drums). They formed a band at school in Dublin in 1977 and constant gigging, including a first visit to

U2

Van Halen

America, helped establish their reputation as live performers. Their major breakthrough came with 'New Year's Day' from 1983's *War* and they continued to gather momentum with *The Unforgettable Fire* (1984). Produced by Daniel Lanois and Brian Eno, it entered the Top 20 in America.

Live Aid proved a pivotal moment in the band's ascension into the major league and their fifth studio album, *The Joshua Tree* (1987), did not disappoint. Again produced by Lanois and Eno, its first three tracks were all hit singles – 'Where The Streets Have No Name', 'I Still Haven't Found What I'm Looking For' and 'With Or Without You'. It went on to sell 25 million copies worldwide.

Rattle And Hum (1988) sold well, giving the band their first UK No. 1 single, 'Desire', while *Achtung Baby* (1991) was a deliberate attempt to forge a new direction, incorporating elements of dance and electronica; the album was lyrically darker than its predecessors.

The ambient *Zooropa* (1993) was recorded between legs of the *Zoo TV* tour and was influenced by its theme of media overkill. The ironically entitled *Pop* (1997) featured familiar themes of love, desire and faith in crisis but was one of the band's lesser-sellers, although 'Discotheque' was a British No. 1 single. *All That You Can't Leave Behind* (2000), reunited the band with producers Lanois and Eno and yielded a UK chart topper in 'Beautiful Day'. Parallel to his band's continuing musical career (a thirteenth studio album was released in 2013), Bono has been increasingly involved in economic/humanitarian concerns.

Steve Vai
(Guitar, b. 1960)

After learning many of his chops from Joe Satriani, New Yorker Vai became Frank Zappa's 'stunt guitarist' on his albums between 1981 and 1986. He was also a hired axe for John Lydon's PiL, Dave Lee Roth and Whitesnake. His own work shows a compositional maturity. Rather than just 'shredding' on *Passion And Warfare* (1990), *Fire Garden* (1996) and *The Ultra Zone* (1999), he experiments and develops moods. And he shreds.

Van Halen
(Vocal/instrumental group, 1972–present)

Van Halen stepped out of California to define the US heavy metal scene for a decade. They boasted a dashing, tuneful frontman, Dave Lee Roth (vocals), a wizard guitarist in Eddie Van Halen and poppy but rocking tunes, as 1978's debut *Van Halen I* proved. Eddie's brother Alex (drums) and Michael Anthony (bass) completed this golden gang. *Van Halen II*

Tom Waits

(1979) consolidated their position, entering the US Top 10, and in 1983 Eddie provided the dazzling solo to Michael Jackson's 'Beat It'. But it was 1984's *1984* and its attendant pop metal smash 'Jump' that promoted the band to the superstar stratum. Roth soon left for a solo career, and Sammy Hagar took over with no effect on chart placings, but a diminution in charisma. When Hagar left in 1996, Roth returned to record two new songs before Extreme's Gary Cherone briefly filled the berth. A reunion tour with Roth took place in 2007 after Eddie's successful battle with cancer, son Wolfgang playing bass.

Stevie Ray Vaughan

(Guitar, vocals, 1954–90)

Born in Dallas, Vaughan distilled Albert King, Jimi Hendrix and Lonnie Mack's blues and rock stylings on his superb US Top 40 album *Texas Flood* (1983). Tommy Shannon (bass) and Chris Layton (drums) formed his trusted Double Trouble back-up team. His ferocious but lyrical playing on *Couldn't Stand The Weather* (1984) and live showmanship confirmed him as the new king of the blues guitar. After a 1990 show with Eric Clapton, Vaughan died in a helicopter crash, but SRV music lives on.

Tom Waits

(Singer/songwriter, b. 1949)

Born in Pomona, California, Waits has built an extremely well-regarded career as a gravel-voiced documentarian of American low-life. The Eagles covered 'Ol '55' from his jazzy debut *Closing Time* (1973). On *Blue Valentine* (1979) and the US Top 100 *Heartattack And Vine* (1980) he introduced a rockier sound. Then came his move into the trailblazing, percussive sounds of *Swordfishtrombones* (1983) and the UK Top 30 *Rain Dogs* (1985), with superb cult musicians such as Victor Feldman (marimba), Marc Ribot (guitar) and Ralph Carney (saxophone). Waits developed a career in soundtracks, including Francis Ford Coppola's *One From The Heart* (1981) with Crystal Gayle, and Jim Jarmusch's *Night On Earth* (1992), and also acted in the likes of *Rumblefish*, *Short Cuts* and *The Fisher King*. His 1999 album *Mule Variations* was a US Top 30 and Rod Stewart made big hits of 'Downtown Train' and 'Tom Traubert's Blues'. His legacy continues to grow.

'The only goal is in the process. The process is the thing … with little flashes of light here and there. Those are the gigs, those are the live shows.'

Jeff Buckley

The Nineties

The Nineties: THE REIGN OF GRUNGE

West-coast city Seattle was the unanticipated epicentre of 1990s music as grunge, the biggest 'back to basics' movement since punk, shook traditional American rock – Nirvana was to enjoy iconic status for a spell until Kurt Cobain's death.

In the UK, the dance rock of The Stone Roses, a holdover from the late 1980s, put Manchester briefly in the picture, but it was American bands like Metallica, The Red Hot Chili Peppers and R.E.M., who had put in nearly a decade of hard graft apiece, whose influential but very different rock sounds gained commercial acceptance at last.

Essential Recordings

1991 Metallica: *Metallica*
Nirvana: *Smells Like Teen Spirit*, *Nevermind*, The Red Hot Chili Peppers: *BloodSugarSexMagik*
1992 R.E.M.: *Automatic For The People*
1995 Oasis: *(What's The Story) Morning Glory?*

The now-dominant influence of MTV made sure the emphasis remained on the visual, while the Britpop 'war' in the mid-1990s saw Blur and Oasis deliver a much-needed kiss of life to a British music business already in a torpor.

1990s acts were not known for their staying power, but the sheer variety of sounds and styles on offer reflected a society where diversity and tolerance were the buzzwords.

Keeping It Real

Technology was about to spawn a powerful rival to music in the affection of the younger generation. The first popular handheld console was launched by Nintendo in 1989, and computer games quickly became the status symbol for anyone under 20. New initiatives were necessary to prevent music from becoming just another teen lifestyle choice like Gameboys, Sega Megadrive and their ilk.

These came in many shapes and from many sources. The Lollapalooza travelling festival kicked off in July 1991 and, staged annually thereafter, would launch many an alt-rocker's career – Nine Inch Nails the first beneficiary. Unusually it was the idea of a musician, Perry Farrell of Jane's Addiction.

Kurt Cobain

MTV, keen to capture the 'mature' rock audience, kicked the *Unplugged* series into gear in January 1990, inviting established acts to bring their acoustic guitars and present their hits in stripped-down form (Eric Clapton's resulting album winning an unbelievable six Grammies).

The singles chart was also coming to an end. This had long been the case in the States, where rankings were now based more on radio airplay than sales, the result being that some hits never actually sold to the public in singles form, being offered to radio only. In Britain, sales would decline year on year until revived by the download-based charts of the 2000s.

The Shape Of Things To Come

For now, it took 'oldies' acts Aerosmith and The Rolling Stones to cotton on to the potential of the internet. In 1994, Steven Tyler and friends released an unissued single for download, while The Stones authorized a 20-minute concert webcast. Comparatively few fans had access to the world wide web at that time, but within a decade these things would be commonplace.

After vinyl and the CD came the MiniDisc – and although it never really became as popular as its predecessors it did help push technologies towards the MP3 player in 1998. This resulted in the mass market making the move from physical media to a file-based system – new music could be consumed at the press of a button. Now the music business faced yet another bout of unwelcome challenges with the arrival of file-sharing on the internet (Napster launched in 1999).

The 1990s was a decade of rapid change – few of the names that dominated the early part of the decade would be conspicuous at its end.

'Americans want grungy people, stabbing themselves in the head on stage. They get a bright bunch like us, with deodorant on, they don't get it.' **Liam Gallagher, Oasis**

Eric Clapton

Headline Acts

Bryan Adams

Bryan Adams
(Singer/songwriter, b. 1959)

This Canadian singer/songwriter first found US success with his third album *Cuts Like A Knife* (1984). With material ranging from pleasing orthodox rock to lung-sucking ballads, the rest of the 1980s were fertile soil especially for rousing singles like 'Summer Of '69'. Adams began the 1990s with the theme song from *Robin Hood Prince Of Thieves*, '(Everything I Do) I Do It For You', which topped the UK charts for a record 16 weeks in 1991. *Waking Up The Neighbours* (1991) and *So Far So Good* (1993) both went multi-platinum and spawned more singles. Although ballads always seem to predominate – on singles and MTV rotation – Adams' roots were never hidden and *18 Till I Die* (1996) was a rousing collection of radio-friendly rock. Adams ended the 1990s where he began with 'When You're Gone', a UK Top 3 duet with Mel C from The Spice Girls. He has concentrated on photography in the new millennium.

Alice In Chains
(Vocal/instrumental group, 1987–present)

This Seattle group, Layne Staley (vocals), Jerry Cantrell (guitar), Mike Starr (bass) and Sean Kinney (drums), cut their teeth on a winning blend of metal and acoustic numbers before being remarketed as a 'grunge' act after Nirvana's huge success. Their second album *Dirt* (1992) won acclaim and huge sales, a position cemented by *Jar Of Flies* EP (1994) and an eponymous third album (1995). Despite spawning imitators, they never realized theirfull potential. Staley died in 2002 of a drug overdose.

The Black Crowes
(Vocal/instrumental group, 1989–2002, 2005–present)

Musically, The Black Crowes were a throwback to the classic rock swagger of The Rolling Stones. Formed in Atlanta, Chris Robinson (vocals), Richard Robinson (guitar), Jeff Cease (guitar), Johnny Colt (bass) and Steve Gorman (drums) combined hard touring and compelling albums such as *Shake Your Money Maker* (1990) and *The Southern Harmony And Musical Companion* (1992). These laid the foundations for a long-term career and extensive chart success, despite a 2002–05 sabbatical.

Damon Albarn of Blur

Blur

(Vocal/instrumental group, 1989–2003, 2009–present)

Formed at London's Goldsmiths College, Damon Albarn (vocals), Graham Coxon (guitar), Alex James (bass) and Dave Rowntree (drums) tuned into the vibe generated by The Stone Roses with baggy anthems 'She's So High' and 'There's No Other Way'. Although *Leisure* (1991) showed a band adept at updating 1960s pop, *Modern Life Is Rubbish* (1993) revealed depth beneath the iceberg of Albarn's pretty face.

With the release of infectious electro single 'Boys And Girls' and the cockney swagger of 'Parklife' Blur found themselves the leaders of the Britpop movement. Albums *Parklife* (1994) and *The Great Escape* (1995) cemented their reputation. Rivalry with Oasis was ill timed, although taking a more loud and experimental approach on *Blur* (1997) and *13* (1999) displayed greater musical maturity without losing sales or fans. Coxon departed to concentrate upon a solo career in 2002. Albarn's desire for wider experimentation and collaboration found full flower in the Gorillaz project.

Jeff Buckley

(Guitar, singer/songwriter, 1966–97)

Son of singer/songwriter Tim, Jeff Buckley possessed an astonishing vocal range, emotional capacity and genuine songwriting talent. His mini album *Live At Sin-e* (1992) was the signpost to the classic debut *Grace* (1994). As well as stellar original material like 'Last Goodbye', Buckley delivered the definitive cover of Leonard Cohen's 'Hallelujah'. Sessions for an eagerly awaited second album ended in May 1997 when Buckley drowned in the Mississippi River. Posthumous releases and acclaim followed.

The Chemical Brothers

(Electronic group, 1989–present)

Initially working under the name The Dust Brothers, Tom Rowlands and Edward Simons began their career as DJs and remixers. After threats of litigation from US Dust Brothers they began recording under the name The Chemical Brothers. Their eclectic, analogue beat-driven dance tracks won a huge following. Live work and collaborations with John Lydon, Noel Gallagher and Beth Orton also displayed their versatility. Albums *Dig Your Own Hole* (1997) and *Surrender* (1999) remain classics.

Creed

(Vocal/instrumental group, 1995–2004, 2009–present)

One of the biggest post-grunge rock acts, formed in Tallahassee, Florida, in 1995, Scott Stapp (vocals), Mark Tremonti (guitar, vocals), Brian Marshall (bass) and Scott Phillips (drums) self-financed their debut album *My Own Prison* (1998). This collection of powerful rock tunes and genuinely spiritual lyrics went on to spawn a record four US No. 1 singles including 'One' and 'What's This Life For'. *Human Clay* (1999) and *Weathered* (2001) followed but troubled Stapps, and the band (now renamed Alter Bridge) agreed to go their separate ways in 2004.

Sheryl Crow

(Singer/songwriter, b. 1962)

The breakthrough hit for this former backing vocalist on Michael Jackson's *Bad* tour was the catchy 'All I Wanna Do', taken off her debut *Tuesday Night Music Club* (1993). However, her eponymous second self-produced album (1996) spawned hits in 'A Change Would Do You Good' and 'Every Day Is A Winding Road'. *The Globe Sessions* (1998) was solid commercial fare. There was a pause before later albums *C'mon C'mon* (2002), *Wildflower* (2005), *Detours* (2008) and *100 Miles From Memphis* (2010).

Scott Stapp of Creed

The Dave Matthews Band

(Vocal/instrumental group, 1991–present)

South African-born Matthews (guitar, vocals) formed his band in Virginia, recruiting Stefan Lessard (bass), Leroi Moore (saxophone), Boyd Tinsley (violin) and Carter Beauford (drums) into the ranks. Fusing elements of world music into a sound that celebrated folk, funk and rock in equal parts, they built an audience by undertaking constant touring, releasing their debut *Remember Two Things* (1993) on their own label.

Now signed to RCA, *Under The Table And Dreaming* (1994) and *Crash* (1996) greatly expanded their US following and led to chart albums. As well as launching a campaign against bootleggers, Matthews released the *Live At Red Rocks 8.15.95* (1997), which showcased the band's compelling stage sound. *Before These Crowded Streets* (1998) was a chart topper and hit single 'Don't Drink The Water' featured Alanis Morissette. On albums like *Everyday* (2001) and *Stand Up* (2006) Matthews' winning compositional ability and band interplay remain undimmed.

Dr. Dre

(Producer, rapper, songwriter, b. 1965)

Adopting the name Dr. Dre, Andre Young is colossally influential in rap. A creative force behind Niggaz With Attitude, he pioneered gangsta rap and has a vast number of production credits, including Snoop Dogg and Blackstreet's 'No Diggity' to his name. Dre also created the more laid-back G-funk musical style. His classic debut solo album *The Chronic* (1992) was released on his own label Death Row Records (1992–96). Dre also discovered and produced Eminem.

Ice-T

(Vocals, b. 1958)

Ice-T, real name Tracy Marrow, grew up in California – his early albums like *Rhyme Pays* (1987) *Power, Power* (1988) and the classic *OG* (1991) showcased his articulate lyrical style.

As well as building a film career Ice-T stretched himself musically with the thrash metal band Body Count, whose track 'Cop Killer' made Ice-T Public Enemy No. 1 to right-wing America in 1992. He is currently working on his ninth studio Ice-T album.

Dave Matthews

Perry Farrell of Jane's Addiction

Jane's Addiction

(Vocal/instrumental group, 1985–1991, 1997, 2001–04, 2008–present)

The charismatic Perry Farrell formed Jane's Addiction in Los Angeles in 1985, Dave Navarro (guitar), Eric Avery (bass) and Stephen Perkins (drums) completing the line-up. Musically the band compacted punk, rock and elements of funk and jazz best showcased on *Ritual De Lo Habitual* (1991). Although Farrell instigated the Lollapalooza travelling festival, the band fractured just as they were hitting the big time in 1991; re-formations in 1997 and 2001 were followed by albums and tours.

Lenny Kravitz

(Multi-instrumentalist, producer, singer/songwriter, b. 1964)

Accused of being 'retro' when first emerging in 1989, Lenny Kravitz proved a trendsetter. Inspired by 1960s icons like Led Zeppelin, The Who and Jimi Hendrix, Kravitz developed a similarly warm, guitar-led sound that became hugely popular. *Mama Said* (1991) and *Are You Gonna Go My Way?* (1993) are prime examples. As well as his own resonant material, Kravitz wrote for other artists, including the sultry 'Justify My Love' for Madonna. He uses a multi-racial/sexual backing band, like Sly and Prince.

Massive Attack

(Dance/vocal group, 1987–present)

Founders and exponents of a downtempo groove of trip-hop, 3D (Robert Del Naja), Daddy G (Grant Marshall) and Mushroom (Andrew Vowles) began working together in Bristol in the late 1980s in a loose collective under the name of The Wild Bunch. Named after a line in a comic book, their debut album *Blue Lines* (1991) introduced this new sound, and with vocal contributions from Shara Nelson and Tricky spawned three hit singles including the masterful 'Unfinished Symphony'. Sought after as remixers, by *Protection* (1994) their sound had matured to a deep dub-laden perfection, made even more compelling with guest vocals from Tracy Thorn (Everything But The Girl) on the title track, as well as Tricky and Horace Andy. *Mezzanine* (1998) was another masterpiece, which, along with trademark soundscapes, featured vocals from Liz Fraser (Cocteau Twins) on 'Teardrop'. Their fifth album *Heligoland* surfaced in 2010 with 3D and Daddy G reunited.

Metallica

(Vocal/instrumental group, 1981–present)

Formed in California in 1981 by drummer Lars Ulrich and James Hetfield (vocals, guitar) the original line-up included Dave Mustaine (lead guitar) and Ron McGovney (bass). However, they soon left and were replaced by Kirk Hammett (lead guitar) and Cliff Burton (bass). This classic line-up laid the foundations of thrash metal with the poorly produced but seminal debut *Kill 'Em All* (1983) and their second release *Ride The Lightning* (1984). Soon snapped up by Elektra Records and with tracks like 'Orion', *Master Of Puppets* (1986) become Metallica's first fully fledged masterpiece. Tragedy struck during a 1986 European tour when Burton was killed. After a decent interval, Jason Newsted was drafted in as a replacement. On their eponymous 1991 album they featured an orchestral backing and shorter, more melodic songs to the trademark hard-edged sound. Seen as a sell-out by some long-term fans, this 'Black Album' became a metal thriller, selling 15 million copies worldwide and spawning five hit singles. It was not until 1996 that a new Metallica album *Load* was released and was as equally commercial as *Metallica*. *Reload* (1997) came hot on its heels and *Garage Inc.* (1998) expanded on the *Re-Visited* EP by offering a full set of covers. Metallica have always been musically sure-footed – to the extent of collaborating with the San Francisco Symphony Orchestra to retool classics for live album *S&M* (1999). In 2001, Newsted left the band and Metallica recorded *St Anger* (2003) with Bob Rock before drafting in bassist Rob Trujillo. Critically mauled, the album was something of a throwback to the early Metallica sound, with the crunching majesty of 'Some Kind Of Monster' clocking in at nine minutes. The traumatic process of recording the album was captured in the film *Some Kind Of Monster* (2004). At the release of their 2008 album *Death Magnetic* they had sold an estimated 100 million records worldwide.

Manic Street Preachers

(Vocal/instrumental group, 1986–present)

When guitarist Richey Edwards disappeared/committed suicide in 1995 the end of the line seemed in sight for this band of Welsh Generational Terrorists. However, James Dean Bradfield (vocals, guitar), Nicky Wire (bass) and Sean Moore (drums) soldiered on delivering *Everything Must Go* (1996). Retaining the artistic integrity that was one of their punk-inspired founding principles, it yielded hit anthem after hit anthem. Subsequent albums were equally compelling as is *The Holy Bible* (1994), recorded before Edwards' presumed death.

Moby

(Instrumentals, producer, vocals, b. 1965)

Making a name for himself on the club scene during the 1980s, Moby's abilities continued to develop throughout the 1990s and were reflected in the chart success of his reworked James Bond theme and album *Animal Rights* (1996). A masterful incorporation of Alan Lomax's field recordings of blues singers was fused into *Play* (1999). 'Why Does My Heart Feel So Bad' was the spearhead single from this album that made him an international Christian vegan superstar.

Alanis Morissette

(Singer/songwriter, b. 1974)

This Canadian singer recorded two teen-oriented albums that went nowhere in 1990 and 1992. Signed to Madonna's Maverick label, major debut *Jagged Little Pill* (1995) was a multi-platinum success. Music aside, it was Morissette's abrasive, honest, sharp lyrical concerns, ranging from anger at being jilted to confessional, that captivated. Singles like 'Ironic' and the Chilis-esque rock power of 'You Oughta Know' were huge hits. Second album *Supposed Former Infatuation Junkie* (1998) spawned 'Thank U' but little else. Drummer Taylor Hawkins joined Foo Fighters.

Alanis Morissette

Nirvana

(Vocal/instrumental group, 1987–94)

One of the most influential acts of the 1990s, Nirvana formed in Aberdeen, Washington, in 1987 when Kurt Cobain (guitar, vocals), Krist Novoselic (bass) and Chad Channing (drums) cemented the line-up.

Seattle's Sub Pop label signed them up and over the next year Nirvana appeared on various compilations and briefly became a four-piece when Jason Everman (guitar) was drafted in for live work. Everman's $600 paid for the recording of Nirvana's debut album *Bleach* (1989). Released in June 1989, the bedrock of the Nirvana sound was evident and with American and European touring, Nirvana began to receive critical acclaim. However, in 1990 Channing departed and Dave Grohl took his place.

Signed by Geffen, Nirvana set about recording a second album with producer Butch Vig. The initial pressing of 50,000 copies of *Nevermind* sold out in two days upon release in October 1991. By now, generational anthem 'Smells Like Teen Spirit' had been released and became Nirvana's first Top 10 single in America and the UK. The follow up 'Come As You Are' established Nirvana as the most celebrated new band in the world and the multi-platinum *Nevermind* became one of the most important and influential albums of the decade.

Classic Recordings

1988 *Love Buzz*
1989 *Bleach, About A Girl*
1991 *Nevermind, Smells Like Teen Spirit, Come As You Are, Lithium, In Bloom, Here She Comes Now*
1992 *Incesticide, Big Long Now, Aneurysm*
1993 *In Utero, Heart Shaped Box, MTV Unplugged In New York, The Man Who Sold The World, Where Did You Sleep Last Night*

Reacting against the commercial sheen of *Nevermind*, sessions for the next album were recorded mostly live in two weeks.

Despite record company objection to the raw sound and pressure that led to the remixing of two tracks, 'Pennyroyal Tea' and 'Dumb', *In Utero* was released as the band intended and topped the charts on both sides of the Atlantic in 1993.

Cobain's state of mind grew darker and, after failing with one suicide attempt, he shot himself in the head at his Seattle home on 8 April 1994. He left a wife, a daughter and a personal legacy that, today, has expanded into iconic proportions.

'We proved that alternative music is a viable commodity.' **Krist Novoselic**

Oasis

(Vocal/instrumental group, 1991–2009)

Mancunian brothers Liam (vocals) and Noel (guitar) Gallagher, Paul 'Bonehead' Arthurs (guitar), Paul 'Guigsy' McGuigan (bass) and Tony McCarroll (drums) signed to Creation Records in 1993. Debut single 'Supersonic' (1994) was a melodic, guitar-driven tune over which Liam snarled out lyrics. By the end of the year another four singles – all instant classics – had graced the charts. *Definitely Maybe* (1994) began a run of 174 weeks in the album charts. Aside from Noel's perfectly constructed pop songs dominated by memorable Beatles-esque choruses, the feuding between the two brothers delighted tabloid editors. This friction did not affect the music, with *(What's The Story) Morning Glory?* (1995) going on to become the second biggest-selling UK album of all time. Although Oasis never cracked America stadium tours of the UK became obligatory and *Be Here Now* (1997) kept the hits coming. Despite personnel changes Liam and Noel buried their differences until a very public 2009 split.

Eddie Vedder of Pearl Jam

Pearl Jam

(Vocal/instrumental group, 1990–present)

Emerging out of former Seattle band Mother Love Bone, the classic line-up consisted of Eddie Vedder (vocals), Stone Gossard (guitar), Mike McCready (guitar), Jeff Ament (bass) and Dave Abbruzzese (drums). The spiky hook-laden rock of *Ten* (1991) sold in large numbers after Nirvana made Seattle alternative bands popular. Touring with the Lollapalooza II circus cemented their position as major players. A reluctance to record promotional videos, release singles or tour did not prevent their second album *Vs* (1993) going platinum. *Vitalogy* (1994) confirmed their position as one of the biggest bands in America. Rather than plough one musical furrow, on subsequent albums like *No Code* (1996) Pearl Jam vastly expanded their musical references to include folk and even world music. In an effort to defeat bootleggers they also released 25 double live albums in 2002, of which five clambered into the US charts, confirming longevity and long-term appeal.

Primal Scream

(Vocal/instrumental group, 1982–present)

Formed in 1982 by Glaswegian Bobbie Gillespie (vocals), the band started crafting material with and for remixers – singles like 'Loaded' and 'Come Together' were 1990 club and chart anthems. However, the band returned to rock with *Give Out, But Don't Give Up* (1994) and further dub-like sonic explorations on *Vanishing Point* (1997). Restless explorations yielded the techno guitar fuzz of *XTRMTR* (2000) and reversion to rock fare on *Riot City Blues* (2006) and *Beautiful Future* (2008).

The Prodigy

(Dance/vocal group, 1990–present)

After releasing the infectious 'Charly', Prodigy mainman Liam Howlett secured acid-house credentials with a series of singles, recruiting dancers Keith Flint and Leeroy Thornhill and singer MC Maxim to distract live audiences from his knob-twiddling. *Music For The Jilted Generation* (1994) displayed wide-ranging styles fused on to the frenetic beats. *The Fat Of The Land* (1997) broke the band worldwide via Flint-sung 'Firestarter', a UK No. 1. *Invaders Must Die* was their 2009 offering.

Public Enemy

(Rap group, 1982–present)

Although Public Enemy began trading pioneering hip-hop in the late 1980s the resonance of their music and message of black empowerment resonated through the entire 1990s. Chuck D, Hank Shocklee, Flavor Flav and the informational Professor Griff delivered seminal third and fourth albums *Fear Of A Black Planet* (1990) and *Apocalypse 91 … The Enemy Strikes Back* (1991). 'Elvis was a hero to most, but he didn't mean shit to me' summed up everything they stood for.

Pulp

(Vocal/instrumental group, 1978–2002, 2011–present)

This Sheffield band secured their first John Peel session when still at school (1981). Pulp then enjoyed/endured over a decade of cult success. Albums and singles pulsed out occasional sounds of potency, with Jarvis Cocker's droll observational lyrics fitting snugly over indie guitars that brushed occasional electronica on tracks like 'My Legendary Girlfriend'. By the time of *His 'N' Hers* (1994) Russell Senior (guitar), Candida Doyle (keyboards), Steve Mackey (bass), Mark Webber (guitar) and Nick Banks (drums) had found a patch of four-leaf clovers and the beginning of chart success. Replacing The Stone Roses at Glastonbury (1995), Pulp's 'Common People' and 'Sorted For E's & Wizz' became anthems. *Different Class* (1995) was just that, spawning hits and turning Cocker into a media darling – especially after his bottom-waving protest at Michael Jackson's 1996 Brit Awards performance. Two further albums, *This is Hardcore* (1998) and *We Love Life* (2001), and a nine-year hiatus followed.

Keith Flint of The Prodigy

Rage Against The Machine

Rage Against The Machine

(Vocal/instrumental group, 1991–2000, 2007–2011)

Formed in Los Angeles by Zack De La Rocha (vocals), Tom Morello (guitar), Tim Commerford (bass) and Brad Wilk (drums), their left-wing lyrics were as polemical as their metallic, rhythmic music. Their eponymous debut album (1992) bottled their live sound and frank social commentary. La Rocha left in 2000, the other members forming Audioslave with Chris Cornell, but RATM re-formed in 2007. Two years later they had a UK No. 1 with 'Killing In The Name' after an anti-*X Factor* campaign.

Red Hot Chili Peppers

(Vocal/instrumental group, 1983–present)

Anthony Kiedis, Michael 'Flea' Balzary, Jack Irons and Israeli-born Hillel Slovak met at school in Hollywood, around 1980.

Signed by EMI, their first two albums failed to make an impact but their third *The Uplift Mofo Party Plan* (1987) did. Slovak died of a heroin overdose in 1988 and Irons quit shortly afterwards – 18-year-old guitarist and fan John Frusciante and drummer Chad Smith were to take their places.

Although recorded in mourning, *Mother's Milk* (1989) was a commercial breakthrough. Switching labels to Warner Bros, Rick Rubin produced their next album, which featured the hit ballad 'Under The Bridge'. The album *BloodSugarSexMagik* (1991) went multi-platinum.

Californication (1999) spawned four hit singles and the Peppers were now one of the biggest international live draws, a position confirmed with *By The Way* (2003). 2006 saw the two-CD whammy of *Stadium Arcadium* and in 2011 *I'm With You*.

R.E.M

(Vocal group, 1980–2011)

Consisting of Michael Stipe (vocals), Peter Buck (guitar), Bill Berry (drums) and Mike Mills (bass) a demo secured the release of 'Radio Free Europe'/'Sitting Still' on the Hib-Tone label, which, in turn, led to a long-term deal with the label IRS. Mini-album *Chronic Town* (1982) was critically received. On debut album *Murmur* (1983) Stipe deliberately listed the song titles in the wrong order on the Stipe-designed album sleeve– a habit continued on early IRS albums like *Fables Of The Reconstruction* (1985).

Michael Stipe of R.E.M

By *Document* (1987) – their fifth album – R.E.M. were the biggest and most imitated band on the American alternative college circuit. In 1987 'The One I Love' became their first US hit single and the frantic 'It's The End Of The World As We Know It (And I Feel Fine)' also entered the US and UK charts.

In 1987 they signed to Warner Bros; their first album was *Green* (1988) and *Out Of Time* (1991) took them to the very top of the big league.

As well as topping the US and UK album charts, addictive singles like 'Losing My Religion', 'Shiny Happy People' and 'Near Wild Heaven' became anthems at the height of the 1990s. The eagerly awaited follow-up *Automatic For The People* (1992) was another classic, yielding an astonishing five hit singles.

Musically, *Monster* (1994) returned to the guitar-heavy early days and kicked off R.E.M.'s first international tour in five years. Recorded during sound checks and stolen moments on a grinding 132-date schedule, *New Adventures In Hi Fi* (1996) was a brave departure. Berry, who had suffered a brain aneurysm, left the band in 1997. R.E.M. remained as essential to the 2000s as they did to the 1980s and 1990s and were deservedly inducted into the Rock and Roll Hall of Fame in 2007.

Snoop Dogg

(Rapper, b. 1971)

The Californian rapper got his lucky break on Dr. Dre of N.W.A.'s solo material.

His own solo career soon ensued with his 1993 debut *Doggystyle*. But his next album *Dogfather* (1996) suffered from media backlash in the wake of Tupac and B.I.G.'s murders. Further albums peddling similar themes turned Snoop into rap royalty, yielding film appearances and an autobiography (2001). Whilst others fell by the wayside Snoop's invention remains strong, especially on *R&G (Rhythm & Gangsta): The Masterpiece* (2004).

Kelly Jones of Stereophonics

Soundgarden

(Vocal/instrumental group, 1984–97, 2010–present)

Like Mudhoney, Soundgarden were another early signing to the Seattle-based Sub Pop label. Chris Cornell (vocals, guitar), Kim Thayil (guitar), Hiro Yamamoto (bass) and Matt Cameron (drums) came on like Led Zeppelin and Black Sabbath chewing metal on early releases like *Badmotorfinger* (1991) and gained success. When Nirvana broke into the big league, the Seattle connection saw the riff-heavy melodic sound of Soundgarden re-marketed as 'grunge'. *Superunknown* (1994) was their finest hour and 10 minutes.

Stereophonics

(Vocal/instrumental group, 1992–present)

Kelly Jones (guitar, vocals), Richard Jones (bass) and Stuart Cable (drums) were friends who formed the band in the Welsh village of Cwmaman. Their obvious chemistry delivered loud, passionate melodic rock dominated by Jones' observational lyrics and full-on delivery. *Word Gets Around* (1997) was a mature set delivering UK chart hits like 'A Thousand Trees', as did the follow-up *Performance And Cocktails* (1999). By *Language. Sex. Violence. Other?* (2005) they were on their third drummer but were established rock stars.

The Stone Roses

(Vocal/instrumental group, 1983–96, 2011–present)

This Manchester band – Ian Brown (vocals), John Squire (guitar), Gary 'Mani' Mounfield (bass) and Alan 'Reni' Wren (drums) – announced their jangling guitar pop with second single 'Sally Cinnamon'. An eponymous debut album (1989) fused the vibe of acid house on to hook-laden melodic hypnotic pop songs. The funk groove of 'Fool's Gold' and anthemic 'One Love' remain untouchable singles. *Second Coming* (1994) fell short of their debut, which is now considered one of the greatest albums of all time.

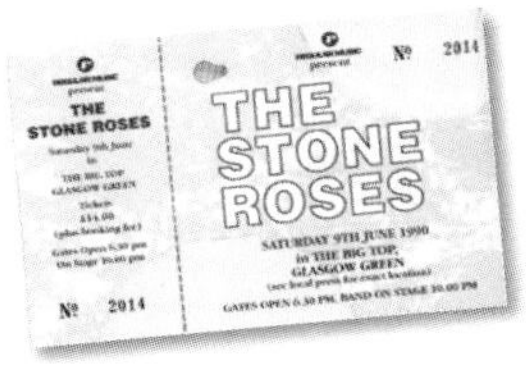

Suede

(Vocal/instrumental group, 1989–2003, 2010–present)

With lead singer Brett Anderson stating 'I'm a bisexual who has never had a homosexual experience', Suede were one of the most exciting bands to emerge in the UK for years. After a startling eponymous debut (1993) and overblown – but masterful – follow-up *Dead Man Star* (1994) guitarist Bernard Butler departed. After recruiting another guitarist and keyboard player *Coming Up* (1996) and *Head Music* (1999) kept the faithful happy without ever fully delivering upon initial promise. Butler and Anderson reunited as The Tears in 2005.

Paul Weller

(Guitar, singer/songwriter, b. 1958)

Weller had already written himself into pop history with the feisty guitar pop of The Jam and soulfully commercial groove of The Style Council when he went solo in 1990. Musically and spiritually renewed by live work, *Paul Weller* (1992) laid strong acoustic foundations for the masterful *Wild Wood* (1994). This mature collection of songs showcased Weller's emotional depth and confirmed a songwriting genius not afraid to explore confessional and pastoral themes. Hit singles as diverse as the tender 'You Do Something To Me' and the rocky 'The Changingman' confirmed his appeal. Although prickly with an adoring media, a strong relationship with adoring younger Britpop musicians from Oasis to Ocean Colour Scene confirmed his influential 'Modfather' status. Always a well-dressed style icon, albums like *Stanley Road* (1995), *Heavy Soul* (1997) and *Studio 150* (2004), on which he tackled a daring array of cover versions, are essential.

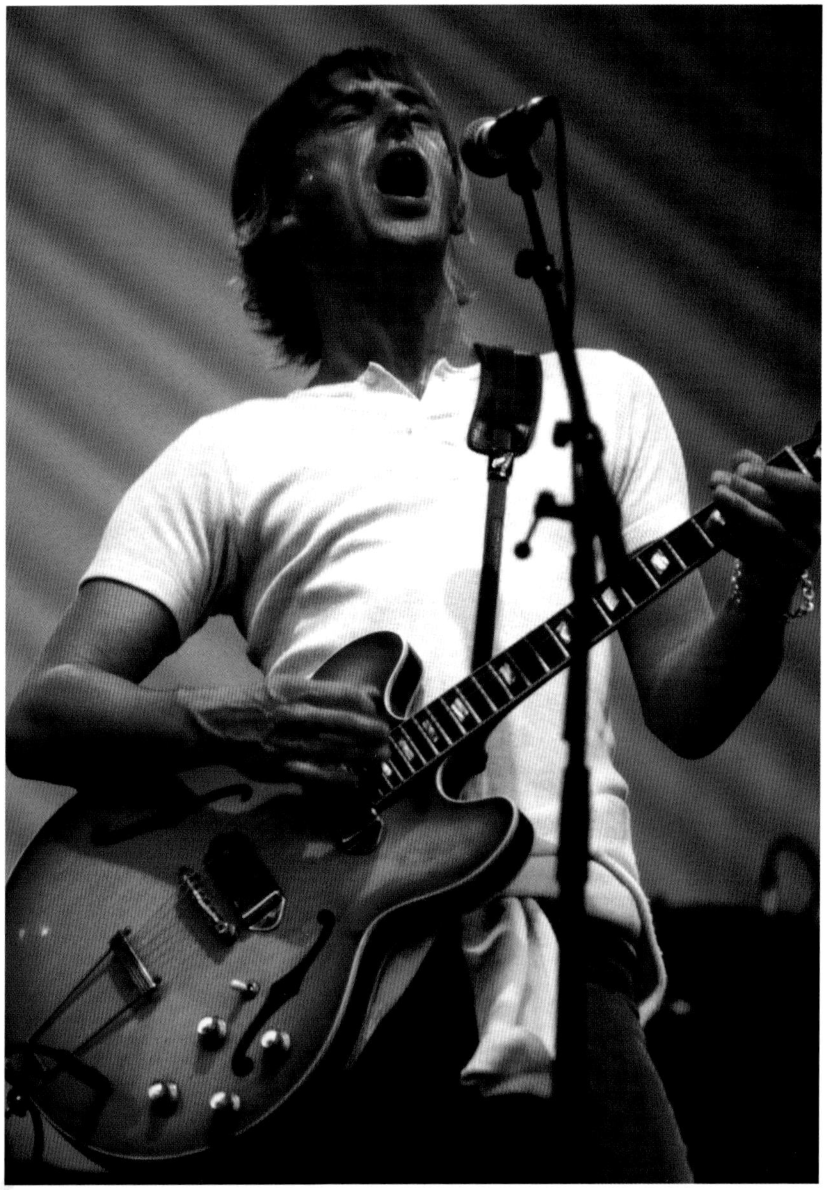
Paul Weller

Robbie Williams

(Vocals, b. 1974)

The former Take That member had numerous hits after leaving the band but it wasn't until *Life Thru A Lens* (1997), which produced the anthem 'Angels', that he was propelled into the super league.

I've Been Expecting You (1998), *Sing When You're Winning* (2000) and *Escapology* (2003) gave us hits like 'Rock DJ' and 'Millennium'. *Intensive Care* (2006) showed a more mature side. After a hiatus he returned to Take That in 2010. His 2012 release *Take The Crown* put him back at the top.

'You can't get that feeling anywhere else. It's communion.
It's like being washed away in the ocean, carried aloft on a wave.'

Pete Doherty on performing

The Twenty-First Century

The Twenty-First Century: ROCK DIVERSIFIES

The impact of rap on the rock market was everywhere to be seen in the first years of the new millennium. White artists, black artists and rock bands attempting to incorporate the style made this area the biggest musical melting pot since the 1950s.

Change For The Good Of Rock?

The means by which music was accessed switched from CD to downloading from the internet, requiring a shift in thinking from a record business already in recession. Yet some of the world's biggest acts remained guitar/bass/drums-oriented. The success of British art rockers Radiohead and Coldplay was probably unsurprising, given the publicity surrounding the re-formation of Pink Floyd for 2005's G8 concert. Add the popularity of Black Sabbath veteran Ozzy Osbourne and it was clear that conservatism still existed.

Essential Recordings

2000 Eminem: *The Marshall Mathers LP*
Radiohead: *Kid A*
2001 The White Stripes: *White Blood Cells*
2005 Coldplay: *X&Y*
2006 Arctic Monkeys: *Whatever People Say I Am, That's What I'm Not*
2008 AC/DC: *Black Ice*

A smattering of punk outrage was supplied by the likes of The Libertines, with original lead singer Pete Doherty, and, more profitably, by Americans Green Day. But even though the world was in turmoil with the events of 9/11 and the terror war that followed, music was now more an escape from reality than a way to make feelings known. Lighting a cigarette at a gig was as rebellious as it got – unless you were Keith Richards, who fell out of a tree when inebriated. Though he survived, the spirit of rock'n'roll was looking distinctly peaky.

Looking Back

In purely musical terms, the century opened with a look back to the future – the biggest-selling album of 2000–01 was *1*, The Beatles' first bona fide greatest hits collection. This sold 3.6 million units in its first week and more than 12 million worldwide in three weeks, becoming the fastest-selling album of all time.

Another return to the 1960s came in the form of manufactured artists, a recurring theme of this century so far, created by shows such as the solo starmaking machines *Pop Idol* (UK) and *American Idol* (the latter's Kelly Clarkson became its first winner in 2002 and was still around four years later, while UK runner-up Will Young proved equally durable) and behemoths like *X Factor* producing the wildly successful Leona Lewis and One Direction. A less expected beneficiary of reality TV was Ozzy Osbourne, the befuddled former Black Sabbath singer, whose household endured the MTV fly-on-the-wall documentary treatment and emerged with superstar status. All of a sudden your idols were obtainable.

Simon Cowell

The Download Generation

Never since the arrival of the black vinyl record had there been a quantum shift in how music was consumed than in the 2000s. While computer games had rivalled music for fans' attention in the 1990s, the new decade saw the personal computer (PC) become the new way to obtain music via downloading. Further to this, the internet was making new stars via its Myspace platform, 2006 UK chart-toppers The Arctic Monkeys and Sandi Thom to name but two. Downloading music not only changed the basis of the pop charts but created a teen status symbol in the shape of the iPod, Apple computers' take on the MP3 player. Apple were among those to start an online music-buying service, iTunes, which sold tracks at affordable prices.

The Killers

With the video revolution still evolving, *Smash Hits*, the teen magazine that had helped a generation of bands to find fame for two decades, closed in 2006. It was the same story with BBC TV's *Top of the Pops*, which ended its 42-year history, swamped by music on demand from innumerable channels. With TV and the net now offering 24-hour access, the days of waiting all week to watch your favourite band were long gone.

'Real' Rock Lives On

Despite the seeming predominance of ephemeral, pop-infused music in recent years, in terms of guitar-based, heavier, harder sounds the 2000s have nonetheless seen the continuation of the 'spirit of rock', as purveyed by such wildly diverse bands as Nickelback, The White Stripes, The Strokes, The Killers, Kasabian, The Hives, Muse, Queens of the Stone Age, Foo Fighters, Green Day, The Arctic Monkeys… The list is endless and ever added to, but reveals the wealth of rock music at our fingertips today.

'There aren't that many things left that haven't already been done, especially with music. I'm interested in ideas that can shake us all up.'

Jack White

Headline Acts

Adele

(Singer/songwriter, b. 1988)

Big-voiced London-born singer/songwriter Adele (born Adele Laurie Blue Adkins) rose from posting a demo on Myspace to a Grammy award in just a couple of years. Her debut LP *19*, released in 2008, reached No. 1 in the UK and No. 10 in the US after an appearance on *Saturday Night Live*; her 2008 single 'Chasing Pavements' was also a big hit. Her blend of white soul and folk proved popular with Americans; she picked up two Grammys in 2009 for Best Female Pop Vocal Performance and Best New Artist.

Arctic Monkeys

(Vocal/instrumental group, 2002–present)

After fans posted early demos of theirs online and created a Myspace profile for them (before the band themselves were even aware of the site's existence), Sheffield's Arctic Monkeys – Alex Turner (vocals), Jamie Turner (guitar), Matt Helders (drums) and Andy Nicholson (bass) – saw their wryly accurate take on northern English life consumed by the public. Their debut album *Whatever People Say I Am, That's What I'm Not* was released in January 2006 and became the fastest-selling album ever in the country, and their breakneck indie soon became a template through which all A&R men looked for new talent.

Arctic Monkeys

Beyoncé

Beyoncé

(Vocals, b. 1981)

Beyoncé Knowles – the surname is rarely used – left Grammy award-winning girl band Destiny's Child in 2003 to pursue the most successful career of any female in the 2000s. Her first solo album, that year's *Dangerously In Love,* went straight in at No. 1 in both the US and UK.

Her follow up, *B'Day*, came three years later in 2006, again topping the *Billboard* 200 and reaching No. 3 in the UK. She made it a hat trick of US chart-topping albums in 2008 with *I Am… Sasha Fierce*, named after her self-proclaimed alter ego that appears when she performs.

She combined her music career, which included five solo US No. 1 singles in the decade, with roles in movies including *Dreamgirls* and *The Pink Panther* (both 2006). She married rap star Jay-Z in 2008 to create black music's golden couple, while sister Solange is next up on father Mathew's conveyor belt of talent. According to record company Sony, her record sales, combined with those of Destiny's Child, have surpassed 100 million.

Blink-182

(Vocal/instrumental group, 1992–2005, 2009–present)

Kings of the snotty, toilet-humoured nu-punk genre, Blink-182 – Travis Barker (drums), Tom DeLonge (vocals) and Mark Hoppus (bass) – formed while at school, recording in their then-drummer Scott Raynor's bedroom. Since then, they have grown older but not matured, with 2001's 'Rock Show' a fine example of the band's awareness of its target audience. They returned from their 'indefinite hiatus' with a 2009 US tour, Travis Barker having survived a plane crash the previous year.

Coldplay

(Vocal/instrumental group 1996–present)

Coldplay were formed in London in 1996 by four college friends – Chris Martin (vocals), Jonny Buckland (guitar), Will Champion (drums) and Guy Berryman (bass). In their early years they played at venues in the Camden area and supported bands they would later go on to shadow and supersede. At this time, the band funded their first record – the much sought-after *Safety EP* CD (1998).

After their responsibilities at university were fulfilled, the band signed a five-album deal with UK label Parlophone, also home to Britpop bands like Blur and Supergrass. After initial internal squabbles were resolved, the band decided to act as a democracy with main songwriter Martin receiving 40% of any profits and the remaining 60% split equally between the other three.

Classic Recordings

2000 *Parachutes, Yellow, Trouble*
2002 *A Rush Of Blood To The Head, In My Place, Clocks*
2005 *X&Y, Fix You*
2008 *Viva La Vida, Viva La Vida*

Parachutes, Coldplay's debut album from 2000, found the band and Martin in good voice, but spectres of college influences still hung over the work – for example, 'Shiver' was strongly influenced by Jeff Buckley, as Martin admitted. Later single smashes from the album, 'Yellow' and 'Trouble', gained them exposure on a worldwide scale.

A Rush Of Blood To The Head, which arrived in 2002, was full of much the same artful musicianship that its predecessor had, but here the band had stretched their wings, honing their live show to one that could fill the largest of stadiums. The clever backwards video of 'The Scientist' gained many awards and plaudits.

By 2003–04 the band began to cite Kraftwerk and the more electronic side of Radiohead as influences, as work for the follow-up album progressed. *X&Y* was finally delivered in 2005 and fans seemed pleased it was not a techno record – although elements of Kraftwerk were evident on single 'Talk'.

Released in June 2008, fourth album *Viva La Vida Or Death And All His Friends* topped the UK album chart and its title track became the band's first US No. 1. As of December 2009, the album was the most paid-for downloaded album of all time, while 2011's *Mylo Xyloto* was the UK's best-selling rock album that year.

Chris Martin of Coldplay

'Coldplay are just four friends trying to make great music.' **Will Champion**

The Darkness

(Vocal/instrumental group, 2000–06, 2011–present)

The Darkness – Justin Hawkins (vocals), Dan Hawkins (guitar), Ed Graham (drums) and Richie Edwards (bass) – are the most unlikely rock stars. Good looks and credibility take second place to stadiums full of fans and steely rock riffs transplanted straight from their heroes, Queen. After wittily titled singles and Christmas offerings, debut *Permission To Land* (2003) sold well. Critics were initially baffled, unsure whether to party or remain aloof. The group split after a water-treading second album without iconic original bass player Frankie Poullain.

Eminem

(Rapper, b. 1972)

Marshall Bruce Mathers III was raised solely by his mother Debbie in Detroit, Michigan in poverty-stricken conditions, which provided ample subject matter for the rapper's lyrical material. He performed from the age of 13, and quickly built a reputation as a skilled wordsmith; increasingly the young Mathers found himself ranking highly as a solo performer in verbal battles with other local rappers. This period is covered in the autobiographical 2002 film *8 Mile* (named after a rough area of Detroit). The film would earn him an Academy Award and Grammy.

A debut album, *Infinite* (1996), recorded while still living with friends and family, was sold from the boot of his car. Rap entrepreneur Dr. Dre discovered Eminem's demo cassette in 1997 and the *Slim Shady LP* was released in 1999. Slim Shady was an alias for Eminem, and a character who represented the more damaged side of the rapper. The album caused a storm of controversy, but the album went triple platinum in its first year. Debut single 'My Name Is' reached No. 2 in the UK charts while 'Stan', a chilling tale of a man driven to murder, went one better.

The next step for Eminem seemed to be to self-reference. *The Marshall Mathers LP* (2000) sold three times as well as its predecessor but, after 2004's *Encore,* his career ran out of steam.

The rapper's career has been constantly plagued by legal battles with his mother (for alleged defamation), two divorces and an ongoing battle with alcohol and drugs. Such events have inevitably had adverse effects on his state of mind, and retirement has often been threatened. He published the 2008 autobiography *The Way I Am* and returned to music in 2009 with *Relapse*, which was named one of the top albums of the year.

Eminem

50 Cent

Flaming Lips

(Vocal/instrumental group, 1983–present)

A longstanding antithesis to manufactured pop, the current incarnation of Oklahoma's Flaming Lips – Wayne Coyne (vocals), Michael Ivins (bass) and Steven Drozd (drums) – plough a decidedly odd furrow, at odds with their more 'traditional' alternative rock past. Now famed for their live performances, which can feature aliens, giant animals, fireworks and prosthetic hands, the music is also innovative, with show tunes, contemporary covers, political rants and beautifully childlike melodies in abundance.

50 Cent

(Rapper, b. 1975)

Curtis James Jackson II was born in New York, and has come to symbolize a brand of rap/actor that somehow manages to place circumstance over actual style. 50 Cent's main claim to infamy is the fact he has been shot numerous times. Understandably brash in his delivery, his thuggish attitude towards many aspects of life, a psychiatrist might add, is a self-defence mechanism.

Either way, after writing for Run DMC in the mid-1990s, 50 Cent found himself without a deal until Eminem and Dr. Dre signed him to their label/publishing company, after hearing him on mixtapes. He is now six albums into his career, the best of which is *Get Rich Or Die Tryin'* (2003), which also titled a film of his life. Produced by Dre, it featured the blunt, syncopated chart hit 'In Da Club' (co-produced by Eminem), a *Billboard* single of the year.

Foo Fighters

(Vocal/instrumental group, 1995–present)

Foo Fighters, the post-Nirvana project of Dave Grohl with Taylor Hawkins (drums), Nate Mendel (bass) and Chris Shiflett (guitar) saw the drummer-turned-singer storm the charts again and again with an honest, workaday approach to rock that was, more often that not, humorously handled. Thankfully too, Grohl could write a melody, and this meant his new band made countless radio hits rather than imitating the obscure punk that had influenced them.

'This Is A Call', 'I'll Stick Around' (both 1995), 'My Hero', 'Walking After You' (both 1997) – the list went on and on, each single more radio-friendly than the last. Often the singles would come backed with hammy promotional films – but while critics accused Grohl of selling out, the likeability of the singer and the quality of his songwriting won through. The band released a *Greatest Hits* in 2009, then went briefly quiet as Grohl played with supergroup Them Crooked Vultures.

Franz Ferdinand

(Vocal/instrumental group, 2002–present)

Glasgow's Franz Ferdinand – Alex Kapranos (vocals), Robert Hardy (bass), Nicholas McCarthy (guitar) and Paul Thomson (drums) – formed from the scene around the city's college of art, but only drummer Thomson actually attended. Many wrongly consider their tightly suggestive brand of 'art rock' to be a result of years spent studying the visual arts, but it more likely stems from their obsession with music's history.

Fans of bands such as The Gang of Four and Fire Engines (even going so far as to release a split single with the latter), the band added in their own twist via slants on the showmen of rock – bands like Queen and Roxy Music. Their winning melodies took them to mainstream acclaim, with their eponymous debut winning the Mercury Music award in 2004 and follow-ups *You Could Have It So Much Better* (2005) and *Tonight: Franz Ferdinand* (2009) peaking at Nos. 1 and 2 in the UK, respectively.

Gorillaz

(Animated vocal group, 1998–present)

Gorillaz, a virtual band created as an antidote to the bland pop its creators (Blur's Damon Albarn and cartoonist Jamie Hewlett) saw dominating the charts, have, through stunning choice of guest vocalists and Albarn's gift for melody, made some of the most memorable pop music of recent years. Their self-titled debut (2001) was comparatively low-key in comparison to its follow-up, but nevertheless held the breezy UK Top 10 hit 'Clint Eastwood'.

2005's *Demon Days* took the four animated characters in the band and coupled them with real-life musical legends, in a glittering ensemble cast that included De La Soul, Ike Turner, Bootie Brown, Neneh Cherry and Shaun Ryder. Singles 'Feel Good Inc' and 'Dirty Harry' saw child choirs, rap artists and Albarn's insightful harmonizing employed to near universal acclaim. The band are also pioneering in their sadly infrequent live performances, utilizing everything from computer graphics to simple shadows to convey the characters without actually revealing the masterminds behind them. 2010 brought *Plastic Beach*.

Dave Grohl of the Foo Fighters

Gossip

(Vocal/instrumental group, 1999–present)

It was the title track from their third album that brought Gossip and larger-than-life frontwoman Beth Ditto to the world's attention. The three-piece dance-rock band – the other members being guitarist Brace Paine and drummer Hannah Blilie – released 'Standing In The Way Of Control' in 2006, which became an indie anthem. Ditto became something of an icon for her body image and aggressively promoted homosexuality.

Beth Ditto of Gossip

Green Day

(Vocal/instrumental group, 1987–present)

Billie Joe Armstrong (vocals, guitar), Tré Cool (drums) and Mike Dirnt (bass) formed Green Day in California in the late 1980s. By 1993 the trio had signed with Reprise, and *Dookie* (1993) was a global success.

1995 saw the release of *Insomniac* and the following year *Nimrod*. The atypical acoustic song 'Good Riddance (Time Of Your Life)' remains a perennial favourite. 2000's *Warning* was a further trek down the road of seriousness.

American Idiot (2004) took them three years to produce. From the melancholy of hit single 'Wake Me Up When September Ends' to the more traditional upbeat, punky sound of the title track, the record proved the band were still relevant and later titled a musical. The *American Idiot* tour took in some of the world's biggest arenas. Nowadays Green Day are seen as innovators, not the bandwagon-jumpers many assumed they were.

P.J. Harvey

(Guitar, singer/songwriter, b. 1969)

Hailing from the UK's 'West Country', P.J. Harvey is now eight albums into her career. Trading in a primeval, highly feminine strain of blues rock, Polly Jean Harvey has moved from stripped-down rock to sophisticated acoustic ballads before a stomping brand of indie that is incendiary when caught live. She has influenced many female acts since the mid-1990s, and has guested and duetted with artists as diverse as Thom Yorke, Nick Cave, Josh Homme and Tricky.

Incubus

(Vocal/instrumental group, 1991–present)

An American rock band from California led by vocalist Brandon Boyd, their style is almost impossible to classify as they draw influences from every conceivable sub-genre of rock, metal, jazz, hip-hop and pop. The band earned mainstream recognition with the release of their 1999 album *Make Yourself*. Several well-crafted albums and singles followed including *Morning View* (2001) and 'Drive', bringing them critical acclaim and further commercial success.

Jessie J

(Vocals, b. 1988)

English singer/songwriter Jessie J (real name Jessica Cornish) began her career writing songs for Miley Cyrus and Chris Brown. Her debut single 'Do It Like A Dude' peaked at No. 2 in the UK in 2010; while her first album *Who You Are* (2011) spawned six Top 10 hits, including the title track 'Nobody's Perfect' and 'Who's Laughing Now'. Her style embraces contemporary R&B, pop and hip-hop and has earned many awards. She was appointed a judge on TV show *The Voice*.

Kaiser Chiefs

(Vocal/instrumental group, 1996–present)

Formerly known as Parva, Leeds' Kaiser Chiefs – Ricky Wilson (vocals), Andrew White (guitar), Simon Rix (bass), Nick Hodgson (drums) and Nick Baines (keyboards) – plough the same indie furrow that fellow Britpoppers Blur did during their *Parklife* era. Wilson, something of an everyman, elicits playful singalong choruses from the most unexpected places, while his band behind him churn out the building, shuddering riffs of singles such as 'I Predict A Riot' and, even more momentously, 'Oh My God'.

Kaiser Chiefs

Kasabian

(Vocal/instrumental group, 1997–present)

Sometimes likened to proletariat rockers Oasis, Kasabian – Tom Meighan (vocals), Serge Pizzorno (guitar), Chris Karloff (guitar) and Christopher Edwards (bass) – hail from Leicester. There is more to the four-piece than a simple rock template, however, with much of the band's sound augmented by multiple vocal sections and a chatter of electronica in the same vein as Primal Scream's mid-period albums. Self-assured, arrogant and growing in stature by the day, Kasabian might well have won over even the harshest detractor.

Keane

(Vocal/instrumental group, 1997–present)

Ever since guitarist Dominic Scott left the band in 1999, Keane – Tom Chaplin (vocals), Tom Rice-Oxley (piano, bass) and Richard Hughes (drums) – have taken the unusual route of not replacing him, supplementing their sound instead with piano. The move proved to be a wise one, as the comparatively unique sound they created has found success.

Formed, like many indie bands, as friends in their home town (Battle, Sussex), the group were lucky enough to score a single deal with Fierce Panda, a label synonymous with tipping major talent for the future. Island Records soon snapped them up, and new material and re-recorded older numbers soon littered the charts. The best example of their work is 'Everybody's Changing', a chiming slice of whimsy that reached No. 4 on its UK re-release in 2004. Third album *Perfect Symmetry* (2008) reached UK No. 1 and was acclaimed by many critics as album of the year.

The Killers

(Vocal/instrumental group, 2001–present)

Vegas' Killers – Brandon Flowers (vocals), Dave Keuning (guitar), Mark August Stoermer (bass) and Ronnie Vannucci Jr. (drums) – were formed from a variety of wanted adverts after Flowers was thrown out of his first band. Influenced by the mass singalongs of Oasis, the technological edge of New Order (their name even came from a fictional band in one of their videos) and the introspection of The Smiths and The Cure, the band found mass acclaim in 2004 with their *Hot Fuss* album.

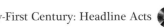

Kings of Leon

Second album *Sam's Town* was released in 2006, and compilation *Sawdust*, containing B-sides, rarities and new material, in 2007. Their third studio album, *Day & Age*, appeared in 2008, and the fourth *Battle Born* in 2012.

Kings of Leon
(Vocal group, 1999–present)

Followill brothers Caleb (vocals and rhythm guitar), Jared (bass) and Nathan (drums) and their cousin Matthew (lead guitar) grew up in Tennessee with the brothers' Pentecostal preacher father. Their first two albums, *Youth And Young Manhood* (2003) and *Aha Shake Heartbreak* (2004), were commercial triumphs, each reaching No. 3 in the UK album charts. Their third LP *Because Of The Times* (2007) hit the UK No. 1 and climbed to No. 25 in the US. A headline slot at the 2008 Glastonbury Festival preceded their fourth album *Only By The Night*, with the lead single 'Sex On Fire', a No. 1 in the UK, typically combining a commercial edge and rock attitude, making them the biggest band in the world. They gained a reputation as one of the hardest-working bands in the business and, although violent sibling rivalries sometimes threatened their future, they have already made their mark on the twenty-first century.

The Kooks
(Vocal/instrumental group, 2004–present)

Brighton's Kooks – Luke Pritchard (vocals), Hugh Harris (guitar), Max Rafferty (bass) and Paul Garred (drums) – are the next in a long line of British acts that can be traced as far back as The Kinks, taking in the likes of Supergrass, Blur and even The Coral on their list of influences. Formed and signed by Virgin on the same night at a gig at a pub in their hometown, they had released two best-selling albums by 2010.

Linkin Park

Lady Gaga
(Vocals, b. 1986)

Stefani Joanne Angelina Germanotta, alias Lady Gaga, made an impact on pop music reminiscent of Britney Spears and Christina Aguilera a decade earlier when her infectious, electronic debut single 'Just Dance' went straight to No. 1 in the UK and US in 2008. The extrovert New Yorker's eccentric fashion style further added to her mystique, and debut album *The Fame* (2008) remained in the chart until the end of the decade. Second album *The Fame Monster* (2009) again reached the UK top spot, and No. 5 in the US, while her over-the-top stage shows became legendary.

The Libertines
(Vocal/instrumental group, 2001–04)

An East London group led by Pete Doherty (vocals, guitar) and Carl Barat (vocals, guitar), who made two albums (*Up The Bracket*, 2002 and *The Libertines*, 2004) of idiosyncratic indie rock produced by The Clash's Mick Jones.

Doherty and Barat presented their songwriting ideas in a ramshackle yet intoxicating way with attitude a-plenty. When the band eventually split in 2004 Doherty, who made headlines for his drug problems, formed the less successful Babyshambles.

Limp Bizkit
(Vocal/instrumental group, 1994–present)

Florida-based Limp Bizkit, led by Fred Durst (vocals), are a global phenomenon. Their fusion of rap with metal (nu-metal) has proved highly influential.

Their second album *Significant Other* (1999) was their breakthrough, and single 'Break Stuff' remains a firm fan favourite. Critical opinion of the band has waned and singles from the third album *Chocolate Starfish And The Hotdog Flavored Water* (2000), such as 'My Way' and the UK chart-topping 'Rollin'', remain the band's high points.

Linkin Park
(Vocal/instrumental group, 1996–present)

Formed from the remains of various Californian college bands and fronted by Chester Bennington (vocals), five-piece Linkin Park are the most successful in the nu-metal genre. Initially called Hybrid Theory, they signed to Warner Bros on the back of a home-produced demo.

Each of their four studio albums since 2000 has reached the Top 3 in the US and their collaboration with rapper Jay-Z, *Collision Course* (2004), topped the chart.

Mumford & Sons
(Vocal/instrumental group, 2007–present)

An English folk-rock quartet from West London led by Marcus Mumford and featuring fellow multi-instrumentalists Ben Lovett, Ted Dwayne and 'Country' Winston Marshall. Their debut album *Sigh No More* (2009) peaked at No. 2 in the UK but topped the charts in Ireland and Australia. They received two Grammy nominations in 2010 and their second album *Babel* (2012) further consolidated their success by topping the charts both in the UK and US.

Muse
(Vocal/instrumental group, 1994–present)

Matthew Bellamy (vocals), Chris Wolstenholme (bass) and Dominic Howard (drums) provide such an enlivening take on the classic power trio formation in rock that it is sometimes easy to forget they are just a trio. Even their earliest singles ('Cave' and 'Muscle Museum', both 1999) were delivered with ferocity and an understanding of what makes a heavy guitar riff exciting – and radio-friendly.

Formed in Cornwall, but building their sound through American influences such as Soundgarden and Nirvana rather than the British ones bands of the time jumped on, Muse were very much outsiders from the start. Albums *Showbiz* (1999) and *Origin Of Symmetry* (2001) saw them stretch rock's confines further, and 2006's UK chart-topping *Black Holes And Revelations* was outrageous, bombastic in its scope and blatant in its nods to rock's past. The self-produced fifth studio album *The Resistance* was released in September 2009 and topped the charts in 19 countries, reaching No. 3 in the US. Critics praised its ambition, classical-music influences and the 13-minute, three-part 'Exogenesis: Symphony'.

Matt Bellamy of Muse

Nine Inch Nails

(Vocal/instrumental group, 1988–present)

Nine Inch Nails – Trent Reznor (vocals), Aaron North (guitar), Jeordie White (bass), Alessandro Cortini (keyboards) and Josh Freese (drums) – are the latest line-up of Reznor's ever-popular band. Somehow walking the thin line between electro and metal, mainstream yet eternally credible, they are one of America's least deified rock bands, but a five-album, double Grammy-winning career shows they are not totally forgotten. Rap superstar Eminem, on debut single 'My Name Is', opted for a closeted reference to the band in the lyrics.

Largely a showcase for Reznor's prodigious multi-instrumental talent, NIN (as it is often abbreviated) found their music reaching the most unexpected of ears when a certain Johnny Cash recorded their 'Hurt' epic in 2004 on the fourth of his hugely appreciated *American Recordings* albums. The death of the country giant less than a year later, and the emotionally draining video, brought legions of new appreciators of Reznor's work.

Queens Of The Stone Age

(Vocal/instrumental group, 1996–present)

Godfathers of the Californian desert rock scene, QOTSA – Troy van Leeuwen (guitar), Joey Castillo (drums), Alain Johannes (bass) and Natasha Schneider (keyboards) – were formed from the ashes of Kyuss by Josh Homme (vocals, guitar), and are one of the heaviest bands on the planet. Sometimes counting Dave Grohl and Mark Lanegan in their ranks (most notably on 2002's *Songs For The Deaf*), their breakthrough came with 2000's *Rated 'R'* featuring the sarcastic anthem 'Feel Good Hit Of The Summer'.

The Raconteurs

(Vocal/instrumental group, 2005–present)

Formed by The White Stripes' Jack White and friend/ songwriter Brendan Benson (along with Jack Lawrence and Patrick Keeler from Detroit's Greenhornes), The Raconteurs fuse White's guitar know-how with Benson's songwriting panache. The concoctions are heady, if openly throwback, and those recorded for debut *Broken Boy Soldiers* (2006) are interesting in the way they were recorded between the main men's projects – and not premeditated, heralded as the work of a supergroup or overly produced.

Thom Yorke of Radiohead

Radiohead

(Vocal/instrumental group, 1985–present)

Oxford band formed (as On A Friday) in 1985 and, as Radiohead, still have the same line-up today: Thom Yorke (vocals, guitar, piano), Jonny Greenwood (lead guitar, effects), Ed O'Brien (guitar, vocals), Phil Selway (drums) and Colin Greenwood (bass). The group's gigging circuit spread south, and EMI, impressed with what they saw, signed the band on a six-album deal. The name Radiohead came from a track on the Talking Heads album, *True Stories*.

Their debut album *Pablo Honey* (1993) included a song called 'Creep', which US radio stations started to pick up on. The band eventually began to resent the track, however. The song 'My Iron Lung' from *The Bends* (1995) obliquely makes reference to 'Creep'.

The 1995 album was Radiohead's most American-sounding, and lyrically it was perhaps their meanest, a sarcastic riposte to the lifestyle unfolding before them.

After *The Bends*, their label was actually happy to wait for the follow-up. The band used a portable studio and set to work on their next album. *OK Computer* was released in 1997 and incorporates themes of escaping, of being trapped and of travel.

By the end of 1997 *OK Computer* was lauded as the greatest album of the year in many publications. Since then, its status has grown steadily.

Radiohead saw no point in replicating what they had achieved with *OK Computer*. The word quickly spread that they might be making a 'techno' record. In fact, they made two. *Kid A* (2000) and *Amnesiac* (2001) were recorded at the same sessions, but released as two separate albums. These sessions had not been easy for the band but much of the material remains as interesting as anything from *OK Computer*.

Meanwhile, other bands began to acknowledge Radiohead as an influence, R.E.M., U2 and Coldplay being chief among them, although Muse, former fans, decided they did not like the band after *OK Computer*. The feeling among the group's fanbase was that Radiohead were finally doing exactly what they wanted. If that meant 'going electronic', then so be it.

With 2003's *Hail To The Thief*, Radiohead fulfilled their EMI contract, and the band issued 2007 album *In Rainbows* on the Internet with no recommended price. It later appeared in physical form to critical acclaim and chart success, debuting at No. 1 both in the UK and in the US.

Over the years, Radiohead, and Yorke especially, have campaigned tirelessly for many causes. At their own concerts they promote the work of Greenpeace and are also staunchly anti-sponsorship, choosing companies to cater their own events that bear no advertising. They also use a low-energy LED lighting system for their performances.

Classic Recordings

1993	*Pablo Honey, Creep*
1995	*The Bends, Street Spirit (Fade Out), My Iron Lung*
1997	*OK Computer, Paranoid Android, Let Down, No Surprises*
2000	*Kid A, The National Anthem, How To Disappear Completely*
2001	*Amnesiac, Packt Like Sardines In A Crushd Tin Box, Pyramid Song, Life In A Glass House*
2003	*Hail To The Thief, 2+2=5, There There*
2005	*I Want None Of This*
2007	*In Rainbows*

'It's a fine line between writing something with genuine emotional impact and turning into little idiots feeling sorry for ourselves and playing stadium rock.' **Thom Yorke**

Rihanna
(Vocals, b. 1988)

Barbados-born R&B sensation Robyn Rihanna Fenty's rise began midway in the 2000s with her debut album *Music Of The Sun* (2005). Her second LP *A Girl Like Me* (2006) made the Top 5 in the US and in the UK, and included hit singles 'Unfaithful' and 'SOS'. *Good Girl Gone Bad* (2007) became Rihanna's most successful album to date on the back of monster chart hit 'Umbrella'. An assault by ex-boyfriend Chris Brown won public sympathy, and fourth album *Rated R* (2009) concluded the most successful five years of any female solo star.

Emili Sandé
(Singer/songwriter, b. 1987)

An English-born Scottish singer/songwriter and radio favourite who debuted on rapper Chipmunk's 'Diamond Rings' (2009), Sandé's first solo single, 'Heaven', was released on Virgin Records in 2011. She has three No. 1 singles to her credit: 'Read All About It' with Professor Green, 'Next To Me' and 'Beneath Your Beautiful', a collaboration with Labrinth. In 2012 she performed in both the opening and closing ceremonies of the London Olympic Games.

Slipknot
(Vocal/instrumental group, 1995–present)

Iowa-based metallers Slipknot – Corey Taylor (vocals), James Root (guitar), Nathan Jordison (drums), Sean Crahan, Chris Fehn (both percussion), Sid Wilson (DJ), Mick Thompson (guitar), Paul Gray (bass) and Craig Jones (samples) – are literally unrecognizable. When playing or posing for photographs, this nu-metal band (very much in the vein of bands like Limp Bizkit but far heavier and less rap-oriented) wear a selection of masks and boiler suits, giving them a menacing anonymity.

Word-of-mouth meant their debut album *Slipknot* (1996) sold close to a million copies and is widely considered their best. Follow-up *Iowa* (2001) saw an almost commercial (for Slipknot) approach to marketing, with the group even appearing as a cameo in the 2002 film *Rollerball*. After a two-year break, the band returned in 2004 with *Volume 3: The Subliminal Verses*, while 2008 brought their fourth studio album, *All Hope Is Gone*, which debuted at the top of the *Billboard* 200.

Rihanna

The Strokes

(Vocal/instrumental group, 1998–present)

Formed after a complicated network of Swiss schooling and gigging frenzy in New York's Lower East Side, The Strokes – Julian Casablancas (vocals), Nick Valensi, Albert Hammond Jr. (both guitar), Nikolai Fraiture (bass) and Fabrizio Moretti (drums) – have come to signify the mass appeal that revivalist bands from the US can achieve. After a bidding war, the band signed to RCA in 2001, releasing *Is This It?*, a short burst of well-trimmed songs and lean riffs. A four-year hiatus preceded their 2010 fourth album.

Sum 41

(Vocal/instrumental group, 1996–present)

Canadian rockers Sum 41 – Deryck Whibley (vocals), Jason McCaslin (guitar), Tom Thacker (guitar, piano) and Steve Jocz (drums) – have struggled to shed the lightweight or 'novelty act' tag that often latched on to them. Certainly earlier albums *All Killer No Filler* (2001) and *Does This Look Infected?* (2002) were high on infantile, skate-punk high jinks, but lately the trio have displayed a more mature, often political side, and seem keen to progress to the second phase of their career, playing benefit concerts and covering John Lennon for charity.

The White Stripes

(Vocal/instrumental duo, 1997–2011)

Divorcées Jack (vocals, guitar) and Meg White (percussion) formed The White Stripes with the mission statement of keeping a childlike simplicity in their music and imagery. Dressing only in red, white and black and playing a thrilling version of blues and rock (owing as much to Led Zeppelin as pioneers like Son House and Leadbelly), the pair found mass international acclaim with third album *White Blood Cells* (2001), which married Jack's jackhammer riffing with a more tender, acoustic side (most notably on single 'Hotel Yorba').

But the duo are far from one-trick ponies. Next album *Elephant* (2003, recorded in a fortnight on a shoestring budget, then receiving massive sales figures) explored multi-tracked vocals, and the follow-up *Get Behind Me Satan* (2005) saw an even darker approach employed, often incorporating marimbas and xylophones. By 2010, their acclaimed output consisted of six studio albums, two EPs, one concert film, 26 singles and 14 music videos.

Amy Winehouse

Amy Winehouse

(Vocals, 1983–2011)

Winehouse's distinctive brand of white soul and R&B rocketed her to fame in 2006 with breakthrough second album *Back To Black*. Public interest in the beehive-hairstyled Winehouse was fuelled just as much by her hedonistic lifestyle as her sultry vocals, but her success, both commercially and critically, was undeniable. The Mark Ronson-produced album won five Grammy awards, and songs like 'Rehab' have become part of popular culture, but her much-publicized addictive personality eventually proved her undoing.

Acknowledgments

Brian May (Foreword)

With a musical career spanning four decades, Queen founding member Brian May is a world-renowned guitarist and songwriter, with production and performance credits on recordings that have sold in excess of 100 million copies worldwide.

Paul du Noyer (Consulting Editor)

Author, editor and music journalist Paul du Noyer began his career on the *New Musical Express*, went on to edit Q and to found *Mojo*. He also helped to launch *Heat* and several music websites, and was an Associate Editor of *The Word*. As well as editing several rock reference books, he is the author of *We All Shine On*, about the solo music of John Lennon, and *Wondrous Place*, a history of the Liverpool music scene.

Contributing Authors

Michael Heatley

Michael Heatley edited the acclaimed *History of Rock* partwork (1981–84). He is the author of over 50 music biographies, ranging from Bon Jovi to Rolf Harris as well as books on sport and TV. He has penned liner notes to more than 100 CD reissues, and written for magazines including *Music Week*, *Billboard*, *Goldmine*, *Radio Times* and *The Mail on Sunday* colour supplement.

Kylie Olsson

Kylie Olsson started her career in TV and Radio working as a presenter and producer for MTV, ITV and the BBC. More recently she has authored *The Art Of Metal*, written sleeve notes for the likes of The Allman Brothers Band and FM and is a journalist for *Classic Rock Presents AOR*. As well as her writing she is also a sought-after TV presenter for Sky Arts and VH1 America, specializing in rock, where she has interviewed some of the biggest names in music and won a prestigious Sony Radio Award for her documentary about John Bonham for the BBC.

Richard Buskin

Richard Buskin is the *New York Times* best-selling author of more than a dozen books on subjects ranging from record production, The Beatles and Sheryl Crow to Princess Diana, Phyllis Diller and Marilyn Monroe. His articles have appeared in newspapers such as the *New York Post*, *The Sydney Morning Herald*, *The Observer* and *The Independent*, and he also writes features and reviews for music magazines around the world. A native of London, England, he lives in Chicago.

Alan Clayson

Musician and composer Alan Clayson has written over 30 books on musical subjects. These include the best-sellers *Backbeat: Stuart Sutcliffe - The Lost Beatle* (subject of a major film), *The Yardbirds* and *The Beatles* boxes. Moreover, as well as leading the legendary Clayson and The Argonauts, who reformed recently, his solo stage act also defies succinct description. For further information, please investigate www.alanclayson.com.

Joe Cushley

Joe Cushley has written extensively for *Mojo*, *Q* and *Uncut* and contributed to several books on music, including *The Rough Guide To The Beatles* and *The Mojo Collection*. He compiles albums for Union Square Music, including the acclaimed *Balling The Jack*, *Beyond Mississippi* and *Definitive Story of CBGB* collections. He is a respected DJ and presents a regular show on London's Resonance FM. Joe is currently Theatre and Books Editor of *What's On In London* magazine.

Rusty Cutchin

Rusty Cutchin has been a musician, recording engineer, producer, and journalist for over 25 years. He began his journalism career in New York as editor of *Cashbox*, the music-business trade magazine. Cutchin has been Technical Editor of *Guitar One* magazine, Associate Editor of *Electronic Musician* magazine, and Editor in Chief of *Home Recording Magazine*. As a recording engineer he has worked on records by artists such as Mariah Carey, Richie Sambora, Yoko Ono, C&C Music Factory, and Queen Latifah. Most recently he has been a consulting editor and contributor to several books on home recording, guitar and music history.

Jason Draper

Jason Draper is the Reviews Editor at *Record Collector*, the monthly music magazine dedicated to collecting music of all genres and on all formats. He has also written for *Uncut*, *Metal Hammer*, *Sound Nation*, *Big Issue Cymru* and *Buzz* magazines.

Hugh Fielder

Hugh Fielder can remember the 1960s even though he was there. He can remember the 1970s and 1980s because he was at *Sounds* magazine (RIP) and the 1990s because he was editor of Tower Records' *TOP* magazine. He has shared a spliff with Bob Marley, a glass of wine with David Gilmour, a pint with Robert Plant, a cup of tea with Keith Richards and a frosty stare with Axl Rose. He has watched Mike Oldfield strip naked in front of him and Bobby Womack fall asleep while he was interviewing him.

Mike Gent

Nurturing an obsession with pop music which dates back to first hearing Slade's 'Gudbuy T'Jane' in 1972, Mike Gent remains fixated, despite failing to master any musical instrument, with the possible exception of the recorder. A freelance writer since 2001, he has contributed to *Writers' Forum*, *Book and Magazine Collector*, *Record Buyer*, *When Saturday Comes*, *Inside David Bowie and the Spiders* (DVD), *The Beatles 1962–1970* (DVD),

Green Umbrella's *Decades* and *The Little Book of the World Cup*. Fascinated by the decade that gave the world glam, prog and punk rock, he is working on a novel set in the Seventies.

Drew Heatley

A writer for the *Nottingham Evening Post*, Drew Heatley was co-author of *Michael Jackson: Life Of A Legend 1958–2009* and *Kings Of Leon: Sex On Fire*, both published in 2009. He has also written books on football, including *Lost League Grounds* and *European Football Stadiums*.

Jake Kennedy

Jake Kennedy is a music journalist from west London. He worked at *Record Collector* for seven years, where he was Reviews Editor. He is the author of *Joy Division & The Making Of Unknown Pleasures*. He writes for numerous magazines and fanzines, and has been a correspondent for Radio 1, BBC 6 and *NME*. He has contributed to Colin Larkin's *Encyclopedia of Popular Music* and the *1001 Albums You Must Hear Before You Die* volume. He is married but never wants kids.

Colin Salter

Since he bought his first single – 'Reach Out I'll Be There' by The Four Tops in 1966 – Colin Salter has spent a life in music as composer, performer, promoter and researcher. His first performance, as panto dame singing ABBA and Supertramp hits in 1975, was succeeded by stints in a Glasgow punk band, a Humberside jazz-folk group and a Kendal jam collective. He worked in theatre for 15 years as a sound engineer and writer of ambient soundtracks. Since 2003 he has been developing a live-music network in rural Cumbria. He moonlights as a golden-oldies mobile DJ.

Ian Shirley

Ian Shirley lived and pogoed his way through British punk rock and has been buying records and watching bands ever since. He is an experienced music journalist whose feature work and reviews appear in respected magazines like *Record Collector* and *Mojo*. He was written the biographies of Bauhaus, and The Residents as well as two science-fiction novels. He has also written the definitive tome on the links between comics and music: *Can Rock And Roll Save The World*. He is currently the editor of *Record Collector's Rare Record Price Guide* and has a collection of over 2,000 vinyl albums and 5,000 CDs.

John Tobler

John Tobler has been writing about popular music since the late 1960s, during which time he has written books on ABBA, The Beach Boys, The Beatles, Elton John, Elvis Presley, Cliff Richard and several generic titles. He has written for numerous magazines including *ZigZag*, *Billboard*, *Music Week*, *Melody Maker*, *NME*, *Sounds*, *Country Music People* and *Folk Roots*. He has written literally thousands of sleeve notes.

Picture Credits

Alamy: Geoffrey Robinson: 187r.

Corbis: A3464 Rainer Jensen/dpa 173t; TOBIAS HASE / POOL/epa 179tr; Andrew Goetz 181; MARIO ANZUONI/Reuters 183.

Getty Images (in page order): David Redfern/Redferns 7, 11, 19l, 44, 54, 57, 59, 60, 62, 70r, 71, 78l, 78r, 79, 104, 118, 120l, 128b, 133l; Paul Natkin/WireImage 8; Rob Carr/Getty Images 9; Blank Archives 10l; Paul Popper/Popperfoto 10r; Peter Still/Redferns 12; Mick Hutson/Redferns 13tl, 152, 153r, 154, 155l, 161, 163r, 165, 185tl; Jan Persson/Redferns 16r, 52, 77r; Rick Richards/Redferns 17l; Chet Atkins/Redferns 18; Michael Ochs Archives/Redferns 28, 17r, 20l, 21, 22, 23, 24, 25, 26l, 27r, 29, 30, 32r, 33, 38l, 42, 43t, 43br, 45b, 46l, 47, 50r, 51, 56, 65, 68, 73c, 76b, 89t, 90tr, 96, 110r, 115, 143; Ian Dickson/Redferns 31, 94, 100l, 101, 113 ; Adam Ritchie/Redferns 36; Gab Archives/Redferns 37; Ralph Ackerman/Hulton Archives 39; Cyrus Andrews/Redferns 40, 49, 63r, 67r, 72 ; Ivan Keeman/Redferns 41tl, 58; David Farrell/Redferns 48l; Don Paulsen/Redferns 53; V&A Images/Harry Hammond 55; RB/Redferns 61; Central Press/Stringer 64; Petra Niemeier/Redferns 66, 75; Echoes/Redferns 69; Michael Ochs Archives 74l, 98; Erica Echenberg/Redferns 82; Graham Lowe/Redferns 83r; Ebet Roberts/Redferns 83l, 85, 92l, 126r, 129, 130, 133r, 135b, 136r, 137, 138, 144, 145, 148; David Warner Ellis/Redferns 84l, 102l, 107, 108t; Richard E Aaron/Redferns 90, 93r, 93l, 114, 116, 119, 123, 147b; Jorgen Angel/Redferns 87tl, 104tr; Michael Putland 88bl; Chris Walter/WireImage 89br; Brian Cooke/Redferns 91r; Richard Creamer/Michael Ochs Archives 97r; Michael Putland/Hulton Archive 99t, 111; Mike Coppola 103tr; Steve Morley/Redferns 103l, 105, 110l; Mike Prior/Redferns 106; Phil Dent/Redferns 109r; Fin Costello/Redferns 121, 86, 87r, 95r, 112c, 117, 122, 131r; Steve Hurrell/Redferns 127; Redferns/Michael Uhll 134l, 139; Bob King/Redferns 135t, 142tl, 156; Rob Verhorst/Redferns 140, 149l, 176t; George Rose/Getty Images 141; Pete Cronin/Redferns 146; Jim Sharpe (Jon Super) 153l; Tim Mosenfelder 157, 186l; Stacia Timonere 158tl; Nicky J. Sims/Redferns 159, 175; Paul Bergen/Redferns 160, 162l; Film Magic/M. Tran/Getty Images 164; Tabatha Fireman/Redferns 166; Patrick Ford /Redferns 167r; Ethan Miller 171; Peter Pakvis/Redferns 172, 174r; Ross Gilmore/Redferns 177; Nigel Crane/Redferns 178; ShowBizIreland/Stringer 179b; Steve Thorne/Redferns 180; Martin Philbey/Redferns 182l; Belgium/Redferns 184.

Photoshot: Dennis Van Tine/LFI: 186r.

Shutterstock: Dja65 12br & 67l; MNI 13tl; Sashkin 13bl & 149tr; Timofeev Sergey 13r; Gallofoto 27l; Bruce Amos 50tl; Mexrix 103br; Tatiana Popova 109l.

TopFoto.co.uk: 170.

And many thanks to the following: Peter (blogger.com/profile/16028212499171228040) 19l; Julien's Auctions 20r; Lacey Siva 26r; elvispresleymusic.com.au 32bl; vicentinedesign.com 41cl; popbotics.com 45t; bradfordtimeline.co.uk 48r; MetalTalk.net 70tl; collectiblesfromthepast 76t; H. Michael Karshis/WikimediaCommons 88tl; glasgowapollo.com 88r; swanseapunk.co.uk 92r; jefflynnesongs.com 97l; ticketcollector 100r; Charles Roffey 112t; jeffverseman.com 131bl; nottinghamrockcity 134r; thepolice.com 142bl; Chiry/planet-dust.laserjay.net 155r; Room237/WikimediaCommons 158cl; www.4q.dk 158r; john-r-james-jr on www.songkick.com 162br; mdmarchive.co.uk/John Squire 167l; jeffverseman.com 173b, 174tc, 182r; flaminglips.com 176b; Steven Gravell 185bl.

Index

Playlists | Links
ebooks & more
FlameTreeRock.com